storytelling
and
creative
drama

18-550-39

storytelling
and
creative
drama

DEWEY W. CHAMBERS
University of the Pacific
Stockton, California

Pose Lamb
Consulting Editor
Purdue University

WM. C. BROWN COMPANY PUBLISHERS
Dubuque, Iowa

literature for children

Pose Lamb
Consulting Editor
Purdue University

Storytelling and Creative Drama—*Dewey W. Chambers, University of the Pacific, Stockton, California*

Illustrations in Children's Books—*Patricia Cianciolo, Michigan State University*

Enrichment Ideas—*Ruth Kearney Carlson, California State College at Hayward*

History and Trends—*Margaret C. Gillespie, Marquette University*

Poetry in the Elementary School—*Virginia Witucke, Purdue University*

Its Discipline and Content—*Bernice Cullinan, New York University*

Children's Literature in the Curriculum—*Mary Montebello, State University of New York at Buffalo*

Copyright © 1970 by Wm. C. Brown Company Publishers

Library of Congress Catalog Card Number: 74-98274

ISBN 0—697—06201—5

Second Printing, 1971

Printed in the United States of America

Art is more godlike than science.
Science discovers . . . . art creates.

PLATO

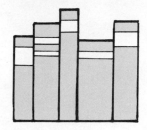

contents

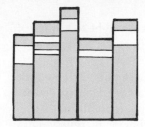

foreword

This series of books came to be because of the editor's conviction that most textbooks about literature for children had not been written for elementary teachers, regardless of the anticipated audience suggested by the titles. The words, *Literature for Children*, preceding each individual title indicate not only the respect for the field held by the authors and the editor but our evaluation of the importance of this type of literature, worthy of consideration along with other categories or classifications of English literature. However, it is *what happens* through books, and the *uses* of literature which are of concern to the authors of this series, as well as the provision of an historical perspective and some knowledge of the writer's and the illustrator's crafts. Our work, then, is directed primarily to the elementary classroom teacher who wants to design and implement an effective program of literature for children.

Because entire books have been devoted to specific topics, for example, the history of literature for children, it is hoped that such topics are covered in greater depth than usual. They are not merely books *about* children's literature; the focus in this series is on helping teachers see what literature for children has been, the direction or directions pointed by scholars in the field, and some ways in which a teacher can share with children the excitement and joy of reading. The authors have tried to share with teachers and prospective teachers their enthusiasm for children's literature, today's and yesterday's; for an unenthusiastic teacher, though well-informed, will not communicate enthusiasm to his pupils.

The author of each book was selected, first because he has demonstrated this enthusiasm in his teaching and writing, and secondly because of his competence in the field of children's literature in general. It is hoped that the thoroughness and depth with which each topic has been explored and the expertise which each author has brought to a topic in which he has a particular interest will serve as sufficient justifications for such a venture.

Children's literature courses are among the most popular courses in the professional sequence at many colleges and universities. It is rewarding and exciting to re-enter the world of literature for children, to experience again the joy of encountering a new author or of renewing acquaintance with a favorite author or a character created by an author.

The editor and the authors of this series have tried to capture the magic that is literature for children and to provide some help for teachers who want to share that *magic with children.*

In Part 1, Storytelling, of his textbook, Dewey Chambers raises some very important issues regarding the literature program, the classroom teacher, and storytelling. Among the questions with which he deals, questions which have occurred to almost every classroom teacher, are these:

> — I have some vague ideas that storytelling can make a contribution to my literature program, but if pressed for specifics by a parent or my principal, I'm not sure what I could say! Exactly *why* is storytelling important? What can it contribute to my program, specifically, the program in literature?
>
> — I agree that storytelling is important and I'm sure my children would enjoy it, but I'm no actor! I *can't!* I'd feel foolish, and nothing would be gained. Could I use tapes or records instead?
>
> — I've never had a course in which storytelling was emphasized, and except for brief presentations before a speech class, I've never had to do this sort of thing. How can I learn this art — or is it a skill — or is some of each involved?

Dr. Chambers writes so persuasively, so enthusiastically about storytelling that readers will move quickly beyond the first 'why' questions and proceed to his discussion of the ways in which one acquires competence in storytelling.

In Part 2, Creative Drama, the author begins with the assumption that creative drama is a natural part of childhood. The task, as he sees it, is that of convincing readers that creative dramatics deserves a more prominent place in the curriculum of the elementary school, the curriculum in literature in particular, than it currently enjoys. The following issues are discussed in some detail, and specific classroom teaching suggestions are given:

> — What preparation is necessary for me? For the children?
>
> — What should I do about makeup, lighting, costumes? Must I

have a stage, or can an effective program be carried on in my classroom?
— What types or forms of literature, what tales, stories, excerpts from books are appropriate?
— Can I evaluate the effectiveness of my program in creative drama? Should pupils be involved in evaluation? If so, how?

Creative drama *is* important. Teachers and pupils will grow, and their programs will be enriched if this facet of the language arts—literature program is effective. Dewey Chambers provides some very effective guidelines for developing a significant program in creative dramatics.

Pose Lamb, Editor

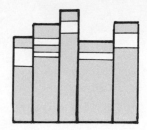

preface

The wonderful world of children's literature is an exciting one. It is a world that is growing rapidly, and it is affecting many thousands of youngsters and their teachers every day. That is good and as it should be. At no time in the history of the world have scholars, editors, publishers, teachers, parents, and librarians been more concerned about the quality of that special art form: the children's trade book. The results of that concern are evident. The quality of children's literature has never been higher.

It seems, however, that this concern has centered mainly on the graphic aspect of the field . . . the syndrome of the printed page. This concentration on the printed page has resulted in the neglect of what is perhaps one very large aspect of children's literature . . . the aspect of children's literature in the oral tradition. The art of the storyteller and the skills required for creative drama have, it seems, been set aside as being perhaps esoteric or else meant for the theatrically talented. If this is true, the field is the poorer because of it.

This book was written as one attempt to correct that possibility. The author, a professional storyteller and teacher of creative drama, strongly believes that the art of storytelling and the skills required to be a successful leader of creative drama are within the grasp of every teacher. *Literature for Children: Storytelling and Creative Drama* will attempt to prove that belief.

In writing this book, the author made every attempt to be practical, pragmatic, and utilitarian. He knows that the busy life of the teacher leaves little time for obscure prose in attempting to learn philosophy and skills that will assist her in the art of teaching. Hopefully, he has succeeded. If he has, the joys of storytelling and the delight of creative drama will be shared with many more children than before.

D. W. C.

section one

storytelling

chapter 1

the oral tradition

Storytelling is the oldest form of literature. This oral literature flourished for thousands of years before print and literacy became common cultural phenomena. Today in the modern world where mass media reaches even the remotest corners, storytellers still exist and practice their art. They practice their art particularly in those cultures where literacy and print are not common cultural tools. But even in those cultures that have utilized the printing press and the marvels of the electronic age, the storyteller still lives and works. This ancient form of literature, literature in the oral tradition, has been and still is, an integral and important part of any society.

In ancient times, the history, the mores, the religion, the customs, the deeds of heroes, and indeed the pride of a people, was transmitted from one generation to another by means of the storyteller. It was he who told of the past, of the adventures of heroes, and the evils of the enemy. It was he who told of gods and devils, of the supernatural, and of magic. The storyteller was a central figure in the fabric of those early societies. Arbuthnot summarizes the importance of the early day storyteller and the tales he told by stating, "folktales have been the *cement of society.* They not only expressed but codified and reinforced the way people thought, felt, believed and behaved."[1]

Not only did the storyteller teach the customs and often the laws of a culture in the ancient times, but he also entertained. He wove the magic net that still captures the imagination of the listener when he told tales for the sake of sheer entertainment. Stories about fictional heroes and their adventures were told and told again. Many became standard-

---

[1]May Hill Arbuthnot, *Children and Books,* 3d ed. (Chicago: Scott, Foresman & Company, 1964), p. 255.

ized and offered hours of escape and beauty to those who could listen. Tales of witchcraft and magic, of noble and brave heroes on adventures beyond the realms of the listener, stories of common folk placed by fate into the role of greatness, tales of mythical lands and beautiful maidens, adventures of animals that lived and spoke like human beings, and stories of the great mysteries that surrounded them became cultural jewels to be heard and passed on to those who had not heard.

The good storyteller was valued by his audience. Often people traveled to his village to hear him tell his tales. Many became famous and were important members of the court of the chief or king. The storyteller's ability with words and imagery, his storehouse of tales, and his ability to tell them were sought after and were much in demand.

The Trade Route

The ancient trader who moved across the land on the routes that offered the best and easiest access to distant towns and trading centers, also had use for the art of the storyteller. When the tired and dusty caravan halted for the evening and sought lodging at an inn, one of the accommodations they most valued was the ability of the inn's resident storyteller. During the meal that the inn offered, or soon after, the storyteller had his time. He told his tales, and with his words helped to erase the weariness accumulated on the trail. Often the storyteller exchanged tales with the guests at the inn. In this way he acquired new stories from distant places for his repertoire. He told not only the old favorites, but newly acquired tales to the traveler, as well.

Folklorists can trace the manner in which certain stories had traveled from one place to another, following their development along an old trade route. The stories had probably changed as they moved along the trade route, but the motif, or the structure of the stories remained intact. The tales probably had been developed in the Middle East, or in Persia, or even in India . . . and had traveled the trade routes, going from storyteller to storyteller, from village to village, ending in Europe or in some other distant place. In the retelling of the tales, the names of the characters probably had been changed in their journey, as well as the clothing they wore, the food they ate, the language they spoke, or the house in which the characters lived . . . but the stories, their motif pattern and their structure, remained the same. It is believed, for example, that the talking beast tales which come to us from the folk treasury of Europe, had their beginnings in India. By the time that these tales about talking animals who lived as human beings arrived in Europe after many years of telling and retelling along the routes of travel, the cultural setting of the tales was vastly different from their cultural setting in India.

The story structure and the motif pattern remained much the same, however.

The stories that emerged in Europe, or that came to Europe from other places, provided a wealth of oral literature for the early European storyteller. Even after the fall of Rome, and with the emergence of medieval Europe, the storyteller continued to ply his trade. The wandering minstrel, the troubadour, and the bard roamed the towns and byways of Europe telling their tales, which often were enhanced by stringed instruments or other accompaniment. They told the old tales, collected new ones, and wrote stories to build up their reputations. Frequently, some of these minstrels banded together, and a traveling troop of storytellers became a band of players versed in another form of storytelling, the drama.

The Christian Storyteller

With the advent of Christianity and its movement to Rome and then to Northern Europe, the message of the church and the story of the Christ was told to the people in the medium of the storyteller. Europe, and indeed the world at that time, was largely populated with illiterate folk. They were unable to read the scriptures and so had to gain the concepts of Christianity in another way, through the oral telling of the message. The Bible and books about the religion were scarce and expensive . . . in that they were handwritten by calligraphers . . . far beyond the grasp of the populace, even if they could have understood the printed word.

What magnificent storytellers those early priests and monks must have been! Their great commitment in telling the story of Christ and his teachings, their great zeal and sincerity in sharing the wonders of this new religion must have taken these men to great heights as storytellers. So accomplished were they that the messages they offered converted the people of the continent to their religion.

The Folktale

The stories of the folk, however, remained the warp and woof of oral literature. Favorite old tales that had been told and told again beside the hearths in countless peasant homes acquired a patina that can come only with well-tended age. New stories emerged from various sources of influential thinking of the times, as well as from the bringing into the cultural milieu a new religion. These new tales challenged the popularity of the old stories.

Superstitions were a favorite topic for the storyteller, too. Witches were burned from their place in the sky with bonfires; dwarfs lived in subterranean kingdoms; evil fairies fought the works of their benevolent sisters; giants roamed the land; and dragons lurked in caves, waiting for the unwary. Ancient gods reappeared in stories, as did the "old magic" of pre-Christian days. *The Golden Bough,* for example, can be directly related to the Christmas Tree . . . giving credibility to the idea that the old stories held such powerful fascination for the people, that this one pagan symbol of the old German tribes has today become a cultural ornament associated with the celebration of the birth of Christ.

These old folk tales, and there were thousands of them, did not remain static when they existed in the oral tradition. Each teller would embellish, change slightly, or add his own touch to the story structure and would expect changes when he heard it from another source. *Rumplestiltskin* of Germany, for example, became *Tom Tit Tot* when he crossed the channel to England. Many other tales made similar metamorphoses.

Storytellers and their tales, in time, took on a kind of nationalistic character. The "wee people," the giants, and the true witch with the pointed hat, for example, seem to have emerged from the British Isles. The trolls, the dwarfs, and the crone are found in great abundance in Scandanavian folk tales. The true fairy, the gossamer maiden who is either good or evil, has much of her background in France. The elves, the wicked witch, the stalwart prince on a white horse seem to be most at home in the forests of Germany. These literary characters are of course found in all cultures. Many students of literature, however, attest to their emergence in certain prescribed environments and, in fact, national boundaries.

main theme

Similar Motif

It is of interest to folklorists and students of literature that certain tales, or at least motif patterns, are found in all areas of the world. Some of these tales are found where social contact between peoples is highly unlikely. Just how these similar tales emerged in such remote places, isolated from each other as they were, remains one of the most intriguing mysteries of literature. *Cinderella,* for example, is found in almost every culture in the world. The *Cinderella* we know is French, and she undoubtedly traveled to France from another source via trade routes or through other contacts with distant peoples. *Cinderella* also was a favorite story of such cultures as the Incas of Peru, the North American Indian, and the Eskimo. She is found in Japanese folk tales and even in stories told on the Islands of the Pacific. To be sure, each culture has a different name for *Cinderella,* and each group does not necessarily have a glass slipper or a grand ball held at the castle. The fairy godmother is often in a different form, and the physical surroundings are very different from those in the Perrault retelling of the tale, but the motif pattern is remarkably similar. May Hill Arbuthnot, the Dean of American scholars of children's literature, pondered this mystery when she wrote, "The three tasks, the flight, the pursuit, the lost slipper or sandal, and the undoing of a spell are found in innumerable racial groups. How were they carried?"[2]

This phenomenon of similar tales emerging in so many remote places, isolated from one another as they were, has given rise to several interesting theories, all of which are worth considering.

The nature myth theory, or man's attempt to explain the mysteries of the natural world around him can, of course, account for many similar tales around the world. Early man often gave inanimate natural phenomena human characteristics. He told tales about these mythical creatures . . . and how they lived and behaved. He created tales about the sun and the moon, the streams, the lakes and the oceans. He explained the clouds and the trees, he accounted for the seasons, the great mountains and the deserts, all with stories that personalized the forces of nature. It is not surprising that similar stories evolved in continents that were distances apart from one another when the motivating stimulus was common to all. The nature myth, and the similarity of natural forces that were their genesis, is one possible reason that folktale motif patterns have similarity throughout the world.

The remnants of ritual from old and forgotten religions can also account for some of the similarity of stories in areas that had little or no opportunity to interchange ideas. Old and forgotten gods and the homage they demanded, regardless of where they were worshipped or what they were called, may account for similar story motifs emerging in lands far apart from one another. Man has always told stories about his gods, and these stories are remarkably alike despite the diverse geographic regions from which they may have come.

Another theory concerning this truth is that man, regardless of where he lives, has similar needs and problems. Certain needs and problems seem to be inherent in our species. Man's attempts to meet these needs and to solve these problems could very likely result in common experiences regardless of where he lives. Early man told stories of how he met these common needs and solved these common problems. It seems evident that a similarity of tales easily emerged on continents oceans apart from each other, when we think of common needs and problems as a genesis for the tales told by early man.

Akin to the theory of man's common needs and problems as a genesis for the tales he told, is the theory that man has similar psychological

---

[2]*Ibid.*, p. 256.

mechanisms regardless of where he is. Many of the tales that come from diverse geographic areas and that are somewhat alike in motif patterns might be explained by this theory. Wish fulfillment, as an example, could explain many of these similar stories. Man's wish to go from a humble station to a station of great renown, or from poverty to great wealth by magic or by supernatural means is a common pattern in folktales from all regions. Man's dream of achieving riches, fame, power, and everlasting youth can produce fantasies in which he can, for a time at least, achieve these goals in the stories he creates. These common psychological dreams or wishes could very well have produced similar tales throughout the world.

The world had a rich literary heritage long before the printed word and the book became a repository for the musings and the creative activity of man. This literary heritage was in the oral tradition, kept alive and ever-growing by the storyteller's art. It was a constantly changing, ever-moving form of literature that was shaped by all that affected mankind. It was not a static form of literature contained intact between the covers of a book. It lived and changed and moved with the people. This literature was of the folk.

Frozen in Print

In 1450, the inventive mind of Johann Gutenberg conceived the idea of movable type. The era of the printing press and mass media had begun. No longer would manuscripts need to be copied by hand; no longer would there be the need for a carefully carved master print block designed only for the reproduction of one page; no longer would printed materials and books be out of reach of the common man. Movable type and the consequent printing press was an invention that literally revolutionized the world. Every man could now interact, through the medium of print, with the musings, the thoughts, and the creative genius of his fellow men.

The stories born in the oral tradition and carried from place to place by the storyteller met the printing press. The storyteller's repertoire contained vast collections of tales which had been changed or modified over the centuries according to location and societal circumstance. These stories were put between the covers of books. The ones that had been such a large part of man's literary heritage because of their unique qualities stopped their natural growth and became frozen in print. They ceased to be a living folk literature and became instead, specimens of folk art.

Avid collectors of these tales performed remarkably well. They soon had gathered together folktales that would, when in print, make their names as famous as the tales they collected. The Grimm brothers, Perrault, La Fontaine, Lang, Jacobs, Asbjörnsen, among others, gathered tales, and as dutiful scribes of folklore, wrote them as they had heard them. These tales were then submitted to the printing press, as they had been written, and have remained the same since . . . frozen in print.

With the invention of the printing press and the subsequent flood of printed materials it produced, there was born the idea that all men have the right to literacy, and the art of the storyteller waned. It still existed to some extent in village kitchens and in meeting halls of remote areas, but, by and large, the book replaced the storyteller as a means of entertaining and communicating ideas.

The old tales that had for centuries lived in the oral tradition now reached new ears through oral reading. Those stories still contained the imaginative magic that was inherent in them, but they remained static . . . unable to change and modify with the times and the setting. They became classic and, at times, even archaic. These tales, born in the oral tradition, were forced to fit the new tradition: literature in print. They have survived, however, and they greet millions of children every year from the pages of books. For a fortunate few, they come to life in their original form . . . as part of the storyteller's special repertoire. It is then that they glow with their special light. It is then that they speak with the clarity of art. The plea of the world's storytellers for the oral tradition in literature is perhaps best stated by that master storyteller, Ruth Sawyer, when she wrote, "There is a kind of death to every story when it leaves the speaker and becomes impaled for all time on clay tablets or the written and printed page."[3] And impaled they are, waiting to come alive again as they were created. They do come alive again, for the storyteller still works, and the magic is still there. Storytelling in our time may be a neglected art, but it is not a forgotten one.

The Ancient Art in a Modern World

Technology is a manifestation of our culture. It is a most welcome one. It is a major innovator in the American classroom. Coupled with the constantly growing body of knowledge about teaching and learning, technology has advanced education to a lofty plain undreamed of a hundred years ago. Today's modern classroom boasts of a multitude of technical marvels to enhance and increase learning. Motion pictures, slide projectors, tape recorders, television equipment, phonographs, overhead projectors, and "teaching machines" are commonplace in most schools and are readily available for use as classroom aids by well-trained teachers. Their effectiveness and value in the learning process cannot

[3]Ruth Sawyer, *The Way of the Storyteller* (New York: The Viking Press, 1965), p. 59.

be denied. The whole world is available instantly, in sight and in sound, to any classroom and teacher.

Unfortunately, this welcome technology has had an effect on the art of storytelling, too. Our technical knowledge has produced an incredible wealth of electronic storytellers who are available to the teacher but who tend to leave him with a fear of competing with them. Many of the old folktales or stories that lend themselves well for telling have been produced by record and film companies with most competent professional actors as storytellers, backed with full orchestras and a battery of special effects experts. The results are often spectacular. Frequently, they are major productions and are well worth the time it takes to listen and watch.

The problem is, however, that these productions are just that— *productions.* They are not, in the real sense, good substitutes for a storyteller. They, of necessity, have missed the essence and issue of the art of storytelling, that of personally relating a good story to a group of listeners at a given time in a given place. Good storytelling, on a one-storyteller, one-group basis, is a highly creative personal experience. It is an experience that develops and glows for a brief period and then disappears. It is an experience that can never be, or ever should be, exactly the same again. Story time is a time of mutual creation, the storyteller and the listener creating together a world built on words and imagination. It is a wonderful, almost secret, private time. Storytelling cannot be mass-produced and still retain its flavor and magic. Teachers need not fear the competition of the electronic storyteller who is a poor substitute for the personal experience that even a novice "real" storyteller can provide.

The ancient art of the storyteller has a valid place in today's modern world. It has a special place that cannot be filled by any reasonable facsimile . . . no matter how polished or how fine. The personal communication that comprises the storyteller's art, the mutual creation between the storyteller and his listener, can exist only when the storyteller and his group meet together and share.

The writer is reminded of an experience he had while visiting an elementary school in central California recently. The fourth grade classroom he visited was as modern and well-equipped as one would expect in a school built only a few years ago in a community that valued its schools and the education of its children. A television set, tape recorder, radio, and phonograph were in evidence. There was a permanent screen for motion picture and slide projection. The library corner held a treasury of children's books, good ones, that were used with obvious regularity. Teaching machines, designed to help students master certain skills, were located on several tables in the classroom. Modern furniture, as well as ample supplies of textbooks, newspapers, and other instructional materials were visible. This classroom, equipped with electronic ventilation and the latest in correct scientific lighting, was as modern as tomorrow, provided as it was with all the available wonders of our scientific age to help children learn.

In spite of this very contemporary background, the teacher was using a technique as old as our language—and yet, curiously, as modern as any of the electronic devices surrounding her. She was telling a story. Her pupils were rapt with attention and were so involved with the creative experience unfolding before them, that they did not notice when a visitor, the writer, entered and sat in the back of the room, where he was soon caught in the web of the storyteller's art.

The woman who stood before the thirty-five or more youngsters was not a trained professional actress. She did not have the colored lights, the music, and the theatrical tricks that one associates with the *professional productions* that children nowadays accept with calm detachment. She was just a teacher, but one who had invested herself in learning the art of storytelling. She told her story with a guileless kind of direct communication. She used the tools of the storyteller's art effectively and well. Her voice was resonant and clear. It moved about the scale emphasizing the mood of the story. It whispered and pleaded, it shouted and whined, it told by its tone and timbre what the listener might interpret. Sometimes she paused, and sometimes she rushed her words, giving an emotional dimension that the children were eager to accept. Her vocabulary was evocative, image-provoking, and exciting. The words she used seemed to leap across to the children and help them form the mental pictures so necessary in a storytelling situation.

Her face, and her eyes particularly, offered another dimension, mirroring the excitement and anxiety of the tale she told. She smiled and frowned with ease. Her eyes, darting about or looking into the distance as if to see a vision beyond, held her listeners firmly under their spell.

Her hands, like the hands of any good storyteller, were a delight to watch and were an important part of her narration. She used them naturally and well, and they added a special spark that gave vividness to her story. Her gestures created much of the magic of the telling by emphasizing, exploring, and asking.

As the tale unfolded, the creative net she wove caught all who were in the room. The story was an old familiar one, one that the children had heard many times before from books and records. But for the first time, *Rumplestiltskin* had come to life for them! He had come to life through the storyteller's art as he was meant to do.

When the teacher finished her tale, and the little dwarf had been thwarted in his evil mission, an obvious sound of approval burst from the thirty-five or more youngsters who had helped to create the story with her. They had been transported to another time and to another place. They had, in their own imaginations, built the castle, clothed the maiden, created the dwarf, and lived with the adventure. It was, indeed, a mutually creative venture . . . the teacher-storyteller providing a genesis for this venture by offering the story in the oral tradition, and the youngsters responding to her skill as a storyteller by creating in their own minds the threads that completed the fabric.

This phenomenon of mutual creativity is perhaps why the ancient art of storytelling still worked its old magic on this group of youngsters. Perhaps in our age of technology, the explicit is so common that the imagination has little opportunity to exercise its potential. In motion pictures and on television, what opportunity to create does the viewer have? In a canned and predigested recording, no matter how slick and professional, the production is predetermined and set . . . unable to change and modify with a group of listeners or to provide a real opportunity for mutual creation. That "special spark," that "indefinable something" which exists between a storyteller and his audience is missing when the story comes from a mechanical device.

In the mutually creative endeavor described above, the teacher-storyteller, of course, played a central part. She created the story . . . the stimulus that resulted in the creative activity of the listeners. She of course knew the story (it was an old familiar folktale), its structure and its sequence of events that produced the problem, the rising action, the climax, the falling action, and the conclusion. She understood and effectively used the storyteller's tools and techniques. The result was a creative act. She modified and changed her story as it progressed with the adventures of Rumplestiltskin and the maiden. She was not giving a "performance." She was sharing this tale as one shares a precious gift with friends. She was aware of and responsive to the children's reactions to the story, pausing effectively when necessary or nodding in agreement with reactions from the group. She would elaborate on a point when she saw the need for it, and she would cut short a point when she saw that the group wanted to move along.

It was an experience that was meant for this particular time, with this particular group, and one that could never be repeated exactly the same way again. She had created a unique, individual experience in storytelling. It was an example of an ancient art flourishing in a modern world, and it was welcomed as an old and trusted friend.

Storytelling is a personal art. It is an art form that demands living human beings as creators, both as listeners and as tellers. It is an art form that lends itself well to technological emulation. When this emulation does occur, however, the product is but a copy. The original is that which is of real value, that which is the true art.

Teachers who are storytellers, therefore, need not fear competition from the electronic storyteller. The productions on records and tapes do have a place in the lives of boys and girls, *but only a place*. These productions must compete with the other technological marvels that children accept with calm regularity. Teachers who can provide the highly personal experience of sharing a good story with children, cannot even be compared to mass-produced electronic storytellers. People, fortunately, are still held in higher esteem than are machines.

The art of storytelling remains one of the oldest and most effective art forms. It has survived the printing press, the sound recorder, and the camera. It will, one might suspect, serve as the means of telling about man's first steps on the planets. The oral story, be it aesthetic or pedagogical, has great value. It seems to be a part of the human personality to use it and want it. The art of the storyteller is an important, valuable ingredient in the lives of children. It has been for thousands of years.

All who tell, or those who have heard, will agree ". . . it seems the art of storytelling is far from dead. It may have moved from the firelit cabin to the fluorescent-lighted classroom or the marble corridors of a museum or some other equally unlikely spot, but the old, old art of storytelling still has power to charm."[4]

Points for Discussion and Things To Do

1. In the stories *Cinderella, Coat of Rushes,* and *Little Scarface,* note the similarity of structure and motif. Can Shaw's *Pygmalion,* and thus *My Fair Lady,* fit into this motif pattern?
2. What old folktales could have had their genesis in:
   a. the nature myth?
   b. old religious ritual?
   c. man's basic needs?
   d. wish fulfillment?
3. Discuss how a story such as *Snow White and the Seven Dwarfs* would be today if the oral tradition had been maintained and the story had not been frozen in print.
4. Listen to a recorded story. What elements are missing to make it a *storytelling* experience?
5. A storyteller operates with the feeling that his art is a mutually creative art. What is meant by a "mutually creative art"?
6. How is oral reading different from storytelling?
7. Are some stories better read than told? How does one decide whether to read or tell?

---

[4]Arbuthnot, op. cit., p. 377.

chapter 2

the story:
guidelines in
selection and preparation

The story is, of course, the heart of any good storytelling experience. Without his tale, the storyteller would not, or could not, exist. The bringing together of the storyteller and the correct story, however, is a curious phenomenon that takes time, knowledge, skill, and sometimes patience. The subsequent preparation of that story is another matter and one that any storyteller needs to consider carefully.

The storyteller literally has the world to draw upon as a source for his stories. He has all literature . . . both in the written and the oral traditions; he has his own experiences and the experiences of others as sources from which to draw as he selects the stories that will comprise his repertoire. The treasure trove of material that is at the storyteller's beck and call would stagger even the most fertile imagination.

The world of folk literature, for example, offers an almost endless supply of tales that beg to be told and still promise the old magic that is inherent in them. Most library collections offer many anthologies of good folk stories. A glance through the volumes by Lang, Jacobs, Courlander, Chase, Asbjörnsen, Harris,* to name just a few, will give an idea of the wealth of folk material available to the storyteller.

Publishers have created handsome volumes of tales from around the world. Exciting tales from India, South America, Japan, Persia, Africa, etc. are readily available.

Early American tales from New England all the way to the camps of the 49ers in the Mother Lode await the storyteller. American Indian stories, stories of the Spanish in the Southwest, stories of the Mountain Men, and stories of the wagon trains all sit waiting in volumes, anxious to be told. The "tall tales," those boisterous, swaggering delights of the

---

*See Selected References at the end of Section 1.

overstatement that characterized our new and restless country, wait impatiently to be heard again. *Paul Bunyan, John Henry, Pecos Bill, Mike Fink, Davy Crockett* . . . all of them are eager to spring to life once more through the storyteller's art.

Whatever the taste, the fare in good folk literature is plentiful. This is the favorite stuff for the storyteller. It is especially good for the beginning storyteller, since folk literature began in the oral tradition and lends itself easily for retelling. These tales have delighted children for hundreds of years and continue to do so today.

With this great amount of material available to the storyteller, the problem of selection is a real one, particularly to the beginning, or novice, storyteller. Even the best and most competent professional storyteller cannot tell every story. He builds his repertoire from tales that are suited to his unique personality and style.

A beginning storyteller must first attempt an evaluation of his own uniqueness . . . his own particular personality . . . his own style. He needs to ask himself, "What kind of stories am I able to tell effectively and well? How can I match my own personality with a tale so that both are able to communicate to the listener?"

Somehow, and no one seems sure as to exactly how, a storyteller *knows* when he has found his tale. Something happens between the storyteller and the tale when he finds it. It seems that the story almost begs to be told by that particular storyteller. It is a story that the teller wants to relate to others. It "clicks" with his personality in such a way that it generates enthusiasm in him that is bound to affect his listeners. Somehow or other, the story fits the uniqueness of the teller. They belong together, this tale and the teller. Storytellers know when it happens. They know they have found a story that belongs to them.

Finding just the right stories for telling does demand time, and sometimes lots of it. First of all, the storyteller needs a rich background of reading. He needs to be familiar with all kinds of story collections and material for good telling before he can identify those that are "just right." The hunting for these stories can be a sheer delight.

The beginning storyteller, who will tell to children, needs to move directly to the children's collection in the library. There he will seek out the volumes that offer the folktales, the anthologies, or the short stories. Then he will begin to read. As he reads, he will note certain tales that offer promise, and he will discard others that clearly are not for his telling. He will note the ones that show promise on 3" x 5" cards or on a note pad so that he can return to them after he has made a more than cursory search of the literature available.

This search for the stories he seeks will take time. It is wise to plan for this. One can't rush this process. It is a personal search . . . a search that cannot be shortened or done in capsule form. If the storyteller knows this and expects to spend time, often that time is a complete joy.

When the teller has found several tales that show "promise" as stories that may belong in his repertoire, he then is ready to return to those stories and make choices. He will likely consider these aspects, among others, as criteria for his selection:

1. Is the story one that personally excites the teller? Is it a tale he wants to share with others?
2. Is it a tale that he *can* tell? Perhaps the content and the mood of the story are not compatible with the personality of the teller.
3. Is the tale one that lends itself to telling? Or would the story be best served if it were read orally to the children, rather than told?
4. Is it a tale that will appeal to the age group of the listeners?
5. Is the length of the tale correct for the audience? Is it too long for young children . . . too short for those in the middle and upper grades?

His selection will depend upon many variables, most of which are subjective in nature. Regardless of how we may try to standardize the teller's selection process, storytelling is still an art, and a highly personal one. And as an art, it often contradicts standardization.

Preparing the Story

After the storyteller has made his selections, he is now ready to go about the business of preparing that story for telling. The preparation of the story for telling is a vital step in moving toward technique. The storyteller needs to keep in mind that he is not doing a "recitation" or a "reading," but that he is telling a story which will live as a unique, singular experience. Memorization is often the first stumbling block to the spontaneity which is necessary in successful storytelling. A good rule is *never memorize a story for telling*. Rather, the storyteller should out-line the content in terms of story structure.

Many folktales, or stories that are good for telling, fall into a cate-gory that dramatists call *melodrama*. Melodrama denotes the structure of a tale . . . how a story is constructed. Usually in melodrama, the opening of the story gives us the *exposition*. It tells us where we are, who is involved, the times, etc. In this introductory exposition, the world is a fairly normal place . . . things are at peace.

In the next step in a melodramatic structure, the *problem* is posed. Here the story really begins. We know that the problem that has been posed must be solved if the story is to have a successful ending. The rest of the story depends upon dissipating the stress caused by the problem.

After the problem has been stated, the next stage in melodramatic structure is that of the *rising action*. The rising action is represented by the efforts of the characters in the story to solve the problem. This rising action, or the efforts to correct the wrong or solve the problem, is often the main body of the story. In terms of time . . . the rising action takes most of it in the storyteller's presentation.

Next comes the *climax* or *denouement*. This is the peak of the story. Here is where the problem is solved, where the wrong is corrected. The climax of the tale is where the excitement that has been mounting in the rising action breaks, and the world of the story can go back to normal. The tension created in the story is released in the climax, and the listener can again relax.

The *falling action* and *conclusion* in a melodramatic story are often told very quickly. This section of the story ties all loose threads, brings the characters back to a peaceful world, and ends the tale so that the listener knows that all is well again.

Needless to say, the structure of the melodramatic story has variations, but essentially it is that of

1. exposition
2. problem
3. rising action

4. climax or denouement
5. falling action, and
6. conclusion

MELODRAMATIC STRUCTURE OF MANY TALES THAT ARE GOOD FOR TELLING

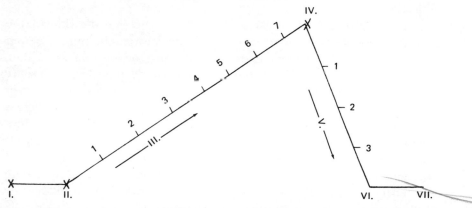

I. Exposition; II. Problem; III. Rising Action (arabic numbers denote incidents; IV. Climax or Denouement; V. Falling Action (arabic numbers denote incidents); VI. Conclusion; VII. End.

Most folktales or other stories that are good for telling, fall into the melodramatic classification. There are, of course, notable exceptions. (See page 17 for a graphic example of this structure.)

In preparing a story for telling, the storyteller needs to keep the structure of the tale constantly in mind. This will help him to decide where to put the emphasis, how much time to spend on the various stages of the tale, and how to break the story into segments that will aid continuity. This awareness of the structure of the story will also help the teller to abstract the tale for his own personal story file.

As a storyteller collects his tales and builds his repertoire, he soon becomes aware of the fact that he cannot rely exclusively on his memory to recall the stories he wants to tell. Many times, the details of an episode become dim in his memory; or, perhaps, specific stages of the rising action are unclear in his mind several months after he first found the story in print. Often, the teller cannot conveniently go back to the specific volume to refresh his memory about the tale. Yet, if he is to tell the tale and be an effective practitioner of the storyteller's art, he must always have the story and its details fresh in mind.

The Story File

One of the most effective ways for the storyteller to assure himself of always having a tale at his immediate disposal, is through the preparation of a story file. This file is made up of abstracts of the stories the teller will use, and is readily available to him whenever he needs to refresh his memory concerning the story, its structure, and its specific episodes.

This file, usually kept on 3" x 5" cards, contains the title of the story, the bibliographic data concerning its location in print, and an outline of its episodes in the exposition, rising action, climax, falling action, and conclusion. This outline uses key words and phrases that are necessary in the telling. It has the characters' names, the sequence of events, and other data that are necessary for the teller to know before he can tell the tale in an accurate, artful way. The outline of the story should be an abstract of the tale, not a rewriting of the entire story. It should contain enough detail to satisfy the teller's needs for recall, but no more. These cards can then be consulted quickly and easily before the teller meets his audience. On these cards is the skeleton of the tale waiting for the teller to add flesh and blood.

Following is an example of this technique of abstracting a tale for telling:

CARD 1

Hansel and Gretel
Watty Piper, ed. *Tales from Storyland.*
New York: The Platt and Munk, Co., Inc., 1941.

I. EXPOSITION
- A. Near a great forest lived a
poor woodcutter with his two
children, Hansel and Gretel, and
their stepmother.

- B. Times were very hard, and a
day came when there was no food
in the cottage except a little
stale bread.

II. PROBLEM
- A. That night, the stepmother told
her husband that it would be
better to take the children out
to the woods where they might find
some berries or roots to eat rather
than starve at home.

CARD 2

- B. The woodcutter was very sad at
the thought of parting with his
children, but he felt that his wife
knew best.

III. RISING ACTION
- A. Hansel overheard his stepmother
and knew what was planned. He
crumbled his bread into pieces,
while Gretel put hers in her pocket.

- B. As they walked along, Hansel
dropped crumbs to mark the path
they were taking.

- C. They found no berries, and at
noon they ate Gretel's bread. It
soon got dark and their father did
not come for them. Gretel began
to worry.

CARD 3

- D. Hansel told her what he overheard. He also told her about the
trail of crumbs he had left. They
would follow it when the moon rose.

E. When they looked for the crumbs,
   they found none. Hungry birds had
   eaten them all. The children fell
   asleep, lost in the forest.

F. Next morning they were awakened
   by a beautiful bird. It seemed to
   call them as it flew from tree to
   tree.

G. All day they followed the bird
   until they saw a cottage. It was
   made of gingerbread.

H. They ran to taste it. The cottage was
   made of many good things to eat.
   An old woman opened the door and
   invited them in to eat.

CARD 4

I. At first they were afraid, but
   they were so hungry they ate all
   she offered.

J. The old woman put them to bed.
   Hansel fell asleep immediately but
   Gretel did not trust the woman and
   stayed awake.

K. The old woman was really a witch.
   She built the house to lure children.
   The witch lifted Hansel from his
   bed and carried him from the room.

CARD 5

L. Next morning, the witch shouted
   to Gretel to get up and fill the
   pail with water from the pump.

M. As she ran out to fill the pail,
   she saw Hansel asleep in a huge
   cage. She called to her brother
   and told him what happened.

N. The whole day, the witch kept
   Gretel busy doing tasks. Finally,
   she told Gretel to heat the oven.

O. Gretel was suspicious for there
   was nothing to bake. When the witch
   told Gretel to crawl into the oven
   to see if it was hot enough, Gretel
   was frightened, for she knew the
   witch wanted to bake her.

CARD 6

P. Gretel told the witch that she
thought she could not get in for
the opening was too small.

IV. CLIMAX
A. The witch argued with her, telling
her that there was lots of room, that
even she could get into it. She
demonstrated how.

B. With that, Gretel grasped the
iron door with both hands and
slammed it against the old witch,
pushing her into the oven.

C. She closed the door and fastened it.

D. The witch shrieked and banged
the door, but Gretel knew she could
not get out for she had left her
magic wand on the table.

CARD 7

V. FALLING ACTION
A. Picking up the wand, Gretel ran
to the cage where Hansel was im-
prisoned, and with one touch of
the magic wand, she opened the door
and set Hansel free.

B. The beautiful bird that led
them to the witch's house flew
down and landed on the ground.

C. It turned into a handsome
young prince. The cage became a
mound of gold and precious stones.

CARD 8

D. It seems that the witch had stolen
the prince from his father's castle
when he was a child and had put
a spell on him that could not be
broken unless a mortal outwitted
the old witch. Gretel had done that.

E. The witch had taken the jewels
and gold when she stole the prince.
The prince gave the children the
gold and jewels as a token of his
gratitude, and went off to find
his father's castle.

F. Hoping to find someone to show
   them the way home, they stuffed
   their pockets with gold and jewels
   and started off.

G. They soon saw their father and
   stepmother coming toward them. The
   parents could not bear the thought
   of the children alone in the forest, and
   came to search for them.

CARD 9

VI. CONCLUSION
A. They all went back to their
   cottage and lived happily and
   never again in poverty. They had
   the gold and jewels and never
   wanted for anything again.

Needless to say, this version of the old German folktale, *Hansel and Gretel,* has been reduced to a skeletal form in the preceding outline. Description, conversation, and details have been removed, and only the main episodes remain. These episodes are placed within the melodramatic structure which will aid the storyteller when he reviews the story prior to actual telling. It is the job of the storyteller to add flesh and blood, clothing, and color to the skeletal outline when he tells the tale. This abstract of an old favorite simply gives the teller the essentials of the story when he needs them. The magic comes later.

A collection of these abstract cards will assure the teller that he has a rich offering for any group. And a storyteller never stops collecting. He finds tales wherever he goes. He collects them on trips, from friends, from family and, most certainly, from the library. It is not uncommon for a successful storyteller to have a story file of more than one hundred tales, ready and at his disposal, for telling.

The storyteller, of course, never takes these cards into an actual storytelling experience, for this would be a distracting element that would not enhance the telling. Rather, he consults the cards before he meets his audience as part of his preparation before telling his tale.

The selection and the preparation of the story are important first steps in developing the art of storytelling. This is the foundation upon which the art is based. The novice or beginning storyteller will find that time spent at this stage of development is time well-invested. The storyteller's material and his preparation of it are major variables for a successful telling. Without this careful selection and preparation, the storyteller is likely to find his experiences with telling somewhat less than successful.

POINTS FOR DISCUSSION AND THINGS TO DO

1. Read a collection of folktales. Note the dramatic structure.
2. Prepare several of your favorite folktales for telling.
3. Notice the dramatic structure of most television programs. Are they melodrama?
4. Where, other than in the library, can good tales for telling be found?
5. Do all tales fall within a melodramatic structure? How would you prepare one that does not?
6. Where, in the structure of a story, should the major dramatic emphasis be placed? Why?

chapter 3

about technique

Miss Hall was a tiny lady. She worked with her fifth grade class in a manner that bespoke her experience, her interest, and her love of children. Her classroom was a place of warmth, efficiency, and productiveness where children appeared to enjoy learning. She was a good teacher. The writer had heard that she was an excellent storyteller too. Accounts of her ability as a storyteller had come to the writer from several sources, and so he determined that it would be good to hear her. He made the necessary arrangements and visited her classroom.

After the writer had been in the room for only a brief period of time, it became apparent to him that Miss Hall had great ability as a teacher. The classroom environment, the children's attitude and productivity spoke clearly of this. But the writer questioned that she had the possibilities for making a good storyteller. Her manner was mild, her voice was extremely soft, and she moved about in a way as to be almost unobserved. Undoubtedly, these traits, or mannerisms, were effective tools for her teaching style, ... but for a storyteller? The writer wondered how this quiet, unobtrusive little woman could possibly hold the attention of a group of listeners and create that special magic that only good storytellers can create. Most of the effective storytellers that he had heard were dynamic personalities who were able to attract the attention of a group simply by their very presence. Their voices were big, their manners at times almost flamboyant . . . they had an air about them that drew interested attention the moment they walked into a room. But Miss Hall? The writer doubted that she had the potential for being a good storyteller.

The classroom activities continued for a few more moments, and finally Miss Hall moved to the front of the room and announced that

John Adams Elementary School. Stockton, California

A classroom setting for storytelling should be informal and relaxed. The storyteller must easily be seen and heard. Setting correct conditions for telling in a classroom is very important.

she had a story to "share" with the children when they were ready to listen. She spoke so quietly and in such an offhand manner that the visitor was not sure all the children heard her. However, they apparently heard her very well. There was a flurry of activity . . . books were put into desks, chairs were moved to suitable places, folders were closed, pencils and pens were put away, and an anticipatory hush settled over the room as the children sat facing their teacher, willing and eager to "share" that story. Miss Hall, sitting on a stool that she had brought out from a closet, waited quietly until the children's busy activity came quickly to an end. Then she began to tell her story.

Nothing very exciting happened while she gave the necessary background of the story so that her audience would know a little about the tale before she began. This tale, we were told, she found the summer before during her vacation in Hawaii. It concerned the *Menehune,* the elves of the Hawaiian Islands. The *Menehune* are favorite topics for Hawaiian stories, and their adventures make exciting listening. Miss Hall showed them a book that she had purchased in Honolulu and told the group that the tale she was going to tell came from this book, *The Tales of the Menehune.*[1] The story she would share with them was called "The Punahou Spring." She casually announced that the book would be in the library corner later so that anyone who wanted to read this story or any of the others in the book could do so.

Miss Hall slipped into the exposition of the story so smoothly that the visitor didn't really know when her introductory remarks ended and the actual story began, but suddenly we had been transported to the island of Oahu in ancient times. We were sharing the concern of an old couple for the dry year that had left the island without enough water. We were being held spellbound at the magic of the *Menehune* who told the old couple, through a dream, how to solve the problem and how the magic spring came into being.

The tale moved so easily and smoothly from exposition, through problem, rising action, and climax, to falling action and conclusion that all of us became involved and created with the storyteller a rare and valuable experience. When Miss Hall finished the story, the murmur of approval and hopeful expectation of more to come was proof enough of her success as a storyteller. She was, indeed, an exceptional teller of tales.

Miss Hall did not move from her stool. Her quiet manner and soft voice remained with her all through the story. She had created a new world, had posed and solved a problem, had made us familiar with a people we had not known before and had stirred our imaginations while quietly sitting on a stool and talking to us. Indeed, Miss Hall knew a lot about storytelling and the techniques of this art.

If the writer had taken the opportunity to quiz Miss Hall about the technique she employed while telling "The Punahou Spring," he would likely have been told about the mechanical aspects of storytelling. She would very likely have discussed the importance of finding a story that she enjoys and wants to share with a group of listeners. She would probably have stressed the necessity to know the structure of the story, how it is built from exposition and problem to falling action and conclusion, and how this knowledge helps the teller reconstruct the story for narration. She might have talked about the physical setting and how

---

[1]Mary Kawena Pukui and Caroline Curtis, *The Tales of the Menehune* (Honolulu: The Kamehameha School Press, 1960).

this variable affects good storytelling. But would she, or indeed, could she, discuss that special quality in her telling that permitted her to sit on a stool and weave her magic as well as she did? This underlying, almost secret aspect of technique is a different matter.

The art of storytelling suggests technique. And yet, most storytellers shrink from this term. Indeed, one well-known author, Ruth Sawyer, devotes one complete chapter in her book, *The Way of the Storyteller,* cautioning storytellers about "technique." Her title for the chapter is aptly named "A Technique to Abolish Technique."[2] The development of the technique of telling, or the development of storytelling style, is so personal, so individual, so unique in each teller that it really defies exact explanation. Yet, if a novice teller is to develop technique, he needs assistance.

Because the art of storytelling is such a highly personal art, and verbal communication is the essence of the art, the selection of the proper story is, of course, the first consideration. The story and the teller must belong to one another.

Miss Hall's "The Punahou Spring" was clearly a tale that she could tell. It matched her personality. Her physical attributes of size and voice, the variables of projection and manner were enhanced by the content of the story she told. As a good and experienced teller, she knew what was best for her. She knew that a storyteller cannot tell all tales. She selected the story to match herself. The telling of a tale is really an expansion of a personality in a dimension that is somewhat different than the usual. If Miss Hall had told a rollicking tale with high, broad humor, or a story that demanded loud and boisterous behavior, she probably would not have been so successful. She simply was not that kind of personality! Telling a tale of high, broad humor would likely have placed Miss Hall in an uncomfortable position. She would have had to rely on tricks, or she might have had to contrive exercises that would have rendered her narration a "performance" rather than a shared art.

Without a doubt, finding the correct story is the first major variable in developing good storytelling style and technique. With a story that does not belong to the teller, the reconstruction of that story in a storytelling situation would very likely become nothing more than a "performance."

The second consideration, the preparation of the story as suggested in an earlier section of this book, is a necessary step in moving toward style and technique. A careful preparation of the correct story in terms of structure, key words and ideas, and mood is the foundation from which style and technique are built.

---

[2]Sawyer, op. cit., p. 131.

Once the story has been chosen and prepared for telling, transmitting that story to the listener in such a way that mutual creation will result is the heart of technique. The storyteller has, after all, only himself and the effective use of words to build his imaginary world. He has no stage setting, no pictures, music, or colored lights to help him create his magic. He must depend upon an effective, expressive voice and clear diction in order to present a rich vocabulary capable of image building. He must use his voice as an instrument that can whisper or shout, that can exude excitement, fear, happiness, or sadness as the story demands. The voice, and the vocabulary it transmits, is a major factor in successful storytelling technique. It is a factor that must constantly be worked on and polished.

A good storyteller is very much aware of words. He knows the value of words and how words can affect a listener. He knows the value of well-placed adjectives and adverbs. He understands the power of the connotative when he selects his words. He knows that, when he describes in his story, he will appeal through words to the senses of touch, taste, and smell. He knows, too, that color, texture, and even temperature can be described in words that could send his listener off on an adventure of imagination. The storyteller is a painter who uses words rather than oils . . . and his pictures, through the artful use of words, are every bit as colorful as are those by his fellow artist whose medium is oil.

The storyteller is not only aware of words and all they can do to the imagination when they are correctly placed and used, but he is also concerned with the way in which words reach the ears of the listener in this oral art. He knows that his voice is a major factor in letting the words he has chosen reach their full potential. The good storyteller avoids the trap of the monotone. The successful narrator utilizes the full scale of tone and timbre that his voice can produce. Shades of meaning and mood can be enhanced, if not created, by the effective use of his voice. The main tools the teller uses to convey his story are his voice and the words it utters. Even the best and most exciting tale can be rendered poorly if the narrator is not careful of the words he uses and the voice that transmits those words.

The body in general, and the face in particular, are also vital aids to the good storyteller. The listener, while hearing the words that build and evoke the images the story provides, watches the storyteller at all times. The teller's face is often the mirror of that story. It reinforces what the listener hears. The good narrator needs a mobile face that is able to frown and smile, to show fear, apprehension, and other emotions that will further the effectiveness of the telling. These facial expressions must be in the mood of the tale, and must never become a caricature unless the tale demands it. They should be natural, not contrived. They should be spontaneous, so as to enhance the telling, rather than a rehearsed collection of "stock expressions" that might have been learned in the old schools of elocution. The face, however, is but one variable in successful storytelling . . . it should not overwhelm or become more important than any other aspect of the art.

The storyteller's eyes are the focal point, for, during the telling, the audience watches his eyes for clues, for emotional expressions, and for reassurance of sincerity. The storyteller watches too. His eye-contact with his listeners can, in a figurative sense, fasten the listeners to the spot and tell them that the story is just for them. During the narration, the effective storyteller will engage the individual members of his audience at eye to eye level as he shifts his direct gaze from one to another. Occasionally, at an important part of the rising action, or at an important segment of the climax, the teller will fix his eyes on one listener or on a group of listeners . . . as if he is sharing this special part of the story with them alone. This technique often gives emphasis to the segment and underscores its emotional impact. The teller will do this only occasionally, however, as giving too much attention to one section of the audience can be a distracting element.

The narrator's eyes can sometimes leave the eyes of the listeners and still maintain an effective mood. A storyteller can often gaze at an imaginary mountain or at a castle behind his listeners as he describes it in the story. So effectively can he focus his eyes on imaginary scenery or on other colorful details, necessitating his breaking direct eye-contact with his audience, that often they will follow his gaze to view with him the imaginative object currently being described in the story. Likewise, should the teller engage in dialogue between two or more characters, it is a point of good technique to establish where these fictional characters stand and then direct the dialogue between them by changing eye-contact. This is often done most effectively by changing the position of the head as well as the eyes when dialogue occurs during the telling.

Storytelling needs to be a personal experience, both from the point of view of the teller and of the listener. The personal aspect of a good storytelling experience is often enhanced and emphasized by eye-contact. Certainly the magic of image building in a storytelling situation is well served if the teller knows that the effective use of his eyes is a major variable in this creative endeavor.

So far, we have noted the importance of the voice and of the choice of words it transmits; we have noted the importance of the face and especially of the eyes of the teller during the delivery of the story. The spontaneous, natural use of the hands in a good storytelling situation is another necessary variable in developing technique.

The hands of a good storyteller are a marvel to watch. His gestures create much of the magic of a good telling by emphasizing, exploring, questioning, and asking. Any discussion of technique must consider the hands of the teller as an essential part of the method of successful telling.

The effective use of the hands often adds an extra dimension to the teller's art. The listener can better understand such aspects as size, distance, texture, and weight through gestures or pantomime with the hands. The gesture undergirds and emphasizes the other points of technique. It adds movement and valuable additional physical aspects to the telling.

The use of the gesture in a storytelling session, like all points of technique, needs to be honest . . . free from the contrived. The gestures must spring from the story, not be an addition to it. Like any other aspect of technique, the gesture should not stand alone as a single effort. Rather, it should be artless in its effectiveness . . . unnoticed in itself, but still an integral part of technique. The wooden or contrived gesture can detract from the story. It looks uncomfortable and unnatural . . . because it is. Gestures, used naturally and well, aid greatly in bringing a story to life.

Technique Combines Many Factors

It is most important to remember that the art of storytelling is achieved by the integration of all points of technique. The effective storyteller will not slight one aspect of technique and emphasize another. It is also important to remember that the teller is sharing a gift with his listeners. He brings it to them with utmost honesty and spontaneity. He is not conscious of tricks and effects of technique and style. He is sharing an art form that must be free from the phony, contrived exercises that are often mistaken for techniques. Perhaps this is why the term "technique" is avoided by most storytellers. Technique or style seems to evolve as a natural part of personality manifestation when the teller is at home with a story or has varied experiences with the art of storytelling.

The beginning or novice storyteller should know that the development of technique or style of telling will take time. With each successive telling, technique and style become more defined. With practice, the skills of telling become more and more a part of the teller. With each experience, the joy of sharing a tale with children becomes more intense and real.

The acquisition of skills of the storyteller does take time. It is an art.

Setting Conditions for Telling

In the Classroom: When a storyteller and a group of listeners meet to create a story, certain psychological and physical conditions need to be considered to insure a successful telling. A classroom setting can be an ideal situation for a story if the teller will remember certain factors.

Storytime needs to be a relaxed, informal occasion. It is a time of sharing, of mutual creation, of beauty. An emotional climate that relates this attitude to the listener must be created by the teller. Many good storytellers do this by simply telling a group that "storytime is a special time, a time of delight . . . a time to relax and enjoy a unique experience."

Usually, too, the good storyteller will instruct children as to how to listen during the time of the telling. In our busy, noisy world, many youngsters do not know how to listen effectively. They need help in learning how to listen so that they can gain all there is to be gained from a storyteller's tale. The electronic storytellers of television, records, radio, and motion pictures have not helped children develop the listening skills they need to interact with a real, "live" storyteller. In fact, many poor listening skills can be directly blamed on these manifestations of our age of mass media. Usually, the teller can quite simply instruct children about listening. He tells the group that this is a time of listening, that it is a time when quiet is important and good listening is necessary, if imaginations are to be switched on . . . if the story they are to hear is to work the magic it can work.

Usually, the storyteller needs to present some background for the story he is about to tell. Sometimes, it can be just a few brief remarks about the tale itself, the author, or the volume from which the story came. At other times, he may want to expand these remarks into a personal commentary about the relationship of the tale to the teller, how he found it, why he likes it, its relevance to the world today, etc. It's not uncommon for the teller to find that the children already know the tale he is going to tell. This is particularly true in the case of folk literature. If the children are familiar with the tale, they can be asked to notice if this version is the same as the one they know. (Most often, they are surprised to find that there is a difference . . . that certain aspects of the tale are different from the version they know.)

If the tale is a familiar one, the teller may indicate to his group of listeners that the story they are about to hear is probably an old favorite of theirs. He does not, however, reveal the name of the tale, but rather tells the listeners that at some point in the story, they will recognize it. He admonishes the listeners to keep this information to themselves until the end of the story, when each can compare with his neighbor as to just when he heard the clue that told him the name of the story.

The location of the listeners in relation to the teller in a classroom situation is an important variable in setting the conditions for effective storytelling. It is most important that the teller be heard easily, and that he be seen without strain. Those two factors, as well as the provision for an informal, relaxed atmosphere, should be facilitated by the proper seating or arranging of a group of children in a classroom setting for a storytime session. Some teacher-storytellers prefer to have the listeners remain in their regular assigned classroom seats. Others like to arrange the group in a different pattern so as to assure an informal, "special" atmosphere that is so desirable to create. Some good tellers like to have their listeners seated in a semicircle in front of them, either on chairs if the classroom provides moveable furniture, or else on the floor. Ways of arranging a group for a telling depend upon several factors, including the teller's personal preference and the physical makeup of the classroom itself. However, the semicircle of listeners sitting in close proximity to the storyteller seems to be most effective, and a favorite way of seating children for a story experience in a classroom setting.

Listeners

Teacher   Storyteller

The semicircle of listeners facing the storyteller in close proximity is an effective way of grouping youngsters for a story experience in a classroom setting.

Out-of-Doors: One of the most effective places for a storytelling experience is out-of-doors. A teller and a group of listeners together in a quiet spot where trees, grass, and sky enhance the teller's art, can result in an experience with storytelling that could reach great heights. The assured informality of an outdoor setting, the relaxing quiet of a verdant spot, will almost always add an extra dimension to the art of storytelling.

Aperture Limited of California, Inc., Stockton, California   John Adams Elementary School. Stockton, California

Telling a story out-of-doors can be a special treat. The environment, however, must be a hospitable one. The setting pictured here is ideal. It provides quiet, shade, and a comfortable place to sit.

Of course, when a storyteller and his group of listeners move out-of-doors, they should do so only if the "out-of-doors" available to them is hospitable. In many settings, particularly in urban areas, the out-of-doors that is available to the storyteller and his group is not conducive to good telling. Certainly, the din of city traffic or the constant rush of a freeway or expressway nearby will render the out-of-doors atmosphere for storytelling less than valuable.

An outdoor setting needs to be quiet, and needs to be a place where the teller and his group can interact without distraction. If this kind of outdoor setting is not immediately available, it is best to remain indoors.

Likewise, the out-of-doors setting should have a climate that is not hostile, that is, one which will not have the distraction of rain, snow, excessive heat, or direct sun glare. The ground area where the children sit must be dry and clean so that clothing, and even health, will not be in jeopardy.

If an out-of-doors setting can be found that is hospitable . . . and there are many available in parks, on playgrounds, in undeveloped areas, etc. . . . . a storytelling session can be a special delight. The right setting and the right time out-of-doors are worth waiting for.

A storyteller who works out-of-doors, will need to modify his techniques somewhat, if he is going to have optimum success with his telling. Certainly, his proximity to his group of listeners will be equally important, if not more so, than when he tells indoors. He no longer can depend upon the variables of walls and ceiling as aids in keeping his group together. The walls and ceiling out-of-doors are the sky and the world all around. The storyteller's voice, when he tells out-of-doors, will need to be stronger than when he tells inside. The voice level he uses inside is enhanced by the enclosing walls and ceiling. When he tells out-of-doors, these do not exist. A teller will need to make sure that his voice does not become lost or ineffective when he works out-of-doors. His voice is a major variable in a good telling . . . and it must be effective outdoors as well as inside.

The seating of a group outside, just as indoors, must provide the listeners with a clear view of the teller as well as an opportunity for easy listening. The semicircular arrangement that has been suggested for indoor storytelling will provide the same rewards in teller-listener rapport if used as an outdoor seating plan. The storyteller out-of-doors will need to guard against the possibility that a member of the group might move behind him while he narrates. This not only can be distracting to the teller and the group, but it can also be unfortunate for the dislocated member of the group who will very likely miss much of the storyteller's art, inasmuch as he cannot directly interact with him.

An outdoor setting for a storytime is highly desirable. The out-of-doors can add a dimension to the experience that will enhance it greatly. The out-of-doors setting should be a hospitable one, however, one that can enhance the telling of the tale. It should not be a distracting element.

At Camp: Probably the most effective setting for a storyteller and his group of listeners is in a camp setting. The built-in informality, the proximity to nature and the primitive world, the togetherness of the group at camp, all add a special, important touch to the mutual creation of a story in the oral tradition. Perhaps a camp setting is such a fine one for the storyteller because it is quite likely that, centuries ago, a similar setting served as the place where the storyteller plied his trade and created the tale. A camp setting removes us from much of the modern world and places us in an environment where this oral art is most at home.

Few settings for the storyteller can equal that of a dark night with woods all around, a campfire that has dwindled to coals, a group of listeners seated around that glowing centerpiece listening intently to the tale, the while building images in the embers. Then the world is much as it was hundreds of years ago, and a tale from the lips of a good teller can exert its unique magic as nowhere else.

Likewise, in the cabin or tent, when the young camper is quiet for the night, conditions are ideal for the storyteller. Here in a new but secure setting, with friends about him, the youngster will listen, and listen again, to the tales the teller will offer. Here, too, the art of the storyteller is at home. Mass media with their programmed stories seem out of place here. They *are* out of place. They cannot compete with this ancient art of literature set forth in the oral tradition in its own setting.

While the camp setting can be ideal, the storyteller needs again to understand that the out-of-doors environment will necessitate some changes or modifications in techniques. A campfire storytime will often produce a large group of listeners, particularly if the word that a story-teller is available spreads about the camp. It is not unusual, at camp, to have upwards of a hundred, and sometimes more, listeners gather at a campfire to hear a storyteller. Needless to say, they must be able to hear and see the teller, and this necessitates a bigger voice, stronger emphasis, and larger gestures on his part than is required of him with a smaller group. Usually, he will have to stand, or else sit on a high stool, so that he is visible to the group. As with any other out-of-door story situation, the variables of an enclosed room do not exist, and the teller will need to accommodate himself to this variable, usually with an enlarged voice and with more definite gestures.

In the cabin or tent, with just a few listeners, the technique, of course, necessitates the opposite. The intimate quality of a cabin or tent group will require the teller to modify his technique to accommodate the listeners there. A softer, more subtle technique than used even in a classroom environment is best in this setting.

The story selections that a teller makes when he offers a tale to a group of children is always important. At camp, it is even more important. The storyteller must be extremely careful in his selections of tales in a camp situation, as the environment is often totally different from any most children have experienced. They are away from home, many for the first time. The people they are with are often strangers to them. While camping is a very valuable experience for children, it can also necessitate difficult adjustment for them.

This writer believes that a storyteller for children should never tell a story that is designed to frighten. Certainly, this is especially true in a camp situation. Children away from home in a strange environment with people they do not know need all the security that can be offered. A storyteller who would tell a story to frighten children should re-evaluate his effectiveness both as a worker with children and as a story-teller. To tell a frightening story to children at anytime, but especially at camp, is not only in extreme bad taste, but is often cruel.

The Tools of the Teller and the Art of Telling

The preparation for and the technique of storytelling suggest honesty, good taste, and quality in this oral literary form. Perhaps these qualities should be more than suggested. Perhaps they should be designated as requirements of and for the working storyteller. As any other art form can be, the art of storytelling can be (and has been) burlesqued. If the art of storytelling is to continue to flourish, then we as storytellers need to maintain our integrity.

As discussed earlier in this section, the storyteller has only his story, himself, and his audience with which to create his magic. His story is one that he has chosen to tell because of its intrinsic literary value and its suitability to his own unique personality factors. He prepares it, utilizing his own personal tools as a teller, that is, his choice of words, his voice, his pace, his gestures, his facial expressions, etc., and sends it to the ears and the imaginations of his listeners. He employs only these elements: (1) a good story, well-prepared, and suited to his particular personality style; (2) the tools of a storyteller, an effective voice and delivery; and (3) the imaginations of his listeners. He should not rely upon, nor employ, tricks or "special effects" that can render his telling a "performance."

The writer is aware of, and has indeed witnessed, that style of storytelling which employs extraneous material in an attempt to enhance a storytime. He has seen the flannelboard used, a chalkboard employed, puppets used; a costumed storyteller; bells and horns clanging and tooting; and once even a live snake slithering over the arms of a teller while he told a tale of why a snake hisses. The writer must confess that, in the latter instance, he never did find out why the snake hisses, so concerned was he that the wriggling specimen would free himself from the teller's arms and invade the audience. (He suspects he was not alone in his concern!)

The writer is impelled to state here that he has never seen an effective storytime, in the sense of true *storytelling*, result from the use of extraneous aids. Each time one of these materials is used, it becomes a distraction, rather than an enhancing agent to the story. The listener naturally becomes very much involved with the material aid, in fact, many times more so than he becomes involved in the story. The entire mutually creative aspect of a good storytelling situation is lost. The storyteller does the creating . . . alone . . . with his aids. The listener loses his chance to create with the teller. His role becomes a passive one . . . he becomes more of a watcher than a listener.

The writer is often tempted to ask a storyteller who employs these gimmicks, why he uses them. What advantage does a teller have when he uses a material aid? What will an extraneous device do to aid the creative art of storytelling? To be quite frank, the storyteller has little or no advantage when he uses a gimmick, and his extraneous device will do little to aid the creative art of storytelling except to act as a distracting element, or to serve as a crutch to the storyteller who lacks the ability to use the art of storytelling in an effective way.

Often these gimmick devices render the telling a "performance." Storytime becomes "show time." These devices often become overly cute, cloying, clever, and a bit saccharine. Their use by a good storyteller is absolutely not necessary.

The art of the storyteller remains one of man's oldest art forms. It is an art form that is particularly valid for children. The adult who tells to children should approach this art with a willingness to invest respect, sincerity, and skill in it. The rewards it offers will far exceed the original investment.

Points for Discussion and Things To Do

1. Discuss the difference between a performance and a storytelling experience.
2. Show, by the use of your voice, how many emotions you can evoke by pronouncing the following words:

   cold   ugly
   dark   beautiful
   satin   granite
   heavy   green
   chocolate
3. Observe people engaged in an interesting conversation. What tools of the storyteller do they employ?
4. Try to carry on a conversation without eye-contact.
5. Assess your own personality and that of a friend in relation to the kind of story each should tell.
6. Analyze your reasons for choosing the stories you have prepared for telling.
7. Tell a story you have prepared to a group of children. Note their reaction. How will you modify the story when you tell it again?

chapter 4

storytelling
and the curriculum

The practicing teacher-storyteller knows that this art form has real and practical application in the ongoing educational program for the elementary school. She knows the value of it as an important way of developing and enhancing the aesthetic education of children. She knows the importance of this art as an aid to children in developing and extending their powers of creativity. As a part of the literature program, storytelling has a unique role to play. Storytelling is *oral* literature . . . a literature that is different from what most children perceive as literature . . . but none the less valid as a form. Children's education in literature would be lacking if storytelling were not a regular part of the curriculum.

The teacher-storyteller knows that the experiences storytelling provides for children in terms of language development are difficult to equal. Storytelling provides an opportunity for children to experience living language, language that communicates at a level above and beyond that of everyday usage. A good storyteller in the classroom is able to provide one of the richest experiences with our language that children can have. The very idea that living words can create a world, pose and solve problems, influence emotions, create images, and provide such delight, is a credit to storytelling's value as a needed part of the language arts program in the elementary school.

While the value of storytelling can easily be seen as a form of literature in children's literary education, and also as a way to enhance the child's language growth through interacting with the storyteller and his tale, this art form is not often viewed as a possible way to undergird other curriculum areas. What an opportunity the teacher is missing if she does not employ the storyteller's art in as many areas of her curriculum as possible. Just the opportunity alone that the storyteller offers children to develop the listening skills (as discussed in Part 2, CRE-ATIVE DRAMA, of this book) makes storytelling an art form worthy of curricular consideration. What a loss to the learner not to have had his education enhanced and brightened by this technique that has been favored by the greatest teachers who have ever lived.

The Social Studies

Next to the language arts, the social studies program is perhaps the field in the elementary curriculum that can best utilize the storyteller's art. This area of the curriculum, concerned as it is with man's adjustment to his physical and social environment, is a natural field for the storyteller. What exciting fare is available to the teacher who tells stories to enhance the social studies.

Any unit in the social studies, from the kindergarten and primary concern with home and family to the upper grade studies of the American frontier and of foreign lands, offers an inexhaustible supply of stories that can be told, thus to make more impressionable the concepts a particular unit is attempting to develop.

Exciting tales from the early American Indians, for example, cannot help but deepen the understanding of the Red Men, how they lived and worked. Their religion, their mores, their fears and hopes are all revealed in the tales they told. Stories from the Latin lands south of our border give us insights into the culture of other Americans living in another part of our hemisphere. Fine tales from Africa, from the Middle East, from the Orient, and from the far North all offer exciting adventures for telling and listening, as well as excellent opportunities to better understand the cultures of these people. Few sources can provide a better understanding of a people than can its literature. Folk literature provides one of the best ways to examine and to understand a society and its culture.

The American adventure, from colonial Boston to the golden Mother Lode, has been chronicled in stories that are waiting to be told. The wagon trains, the flat boats, the early trains, all offer material that lends itself well to telling. Such exciting collections as

BEALS, FRANK L. *Cowboys and Cattle Trails*. Chicago: Wheeler Publishing Co., 1943.

BLAIR, WALTER. *Tall Tale America*. New York: Coward-McCann Inc., 1944.

COY, HAROLD. *The Americans*. Boston: Little, Brown and Company, 1958.

HAYNES, BESSIE D. and EDGAR. *The Grizzly Bear: Portraits from Life*. Norman: University of Oklahoma Press, 1966.

LEACH, MARIA. *The Rainbow Book of American Folktales and Legends*. New York: The World Publishing Co., 1958.

Aperture Limited of California, Inc., Stockton,   John Adams Elementary School. Stockton, California
California   fornia

Listening to an exciting tale told by a good storyteller is a rare and valuable experience. The storyteller's magic can set imaginations spinning.
Images of strange and wonderful worlds are built by this mutually
creative art.

RUSHMORE, HELEN, and HUNT, WOLF ROBE. *The Dancing Horses of Acoma.* New York: The World Publishing Co., 1963.

among many, many others (see Selected References at the end of this section) offer a bonanza of tales waiting to be told by the storyteller.

The mysteries of time and space, the solving of real problems, the personal involvement in history, all take on new meaning and interest when a storyteller works with material from the social studies. Famous, and sometimes not so famous, figures in history offer thrilling adventures for storytelling. George Washington, Abraham Lincoln, Betsy Ross, Thomas Edison, and even Jesse James are material for good stories that reveal the life and times of another age. The sometimes dreary textbook does not always offer the adventure and the extra dimension that the storyteller can offer. So far as a means of presenting content in the curriculum effectively is concerned, the good storyteller is without peer.

Children derive a vicarious thrill when, through the magic of a storyteller's art, they can don buckskins or gingham and ride the covered wagons. They enjoy and they *learn* when they hear the magic tales of ancient Japan. The stories of the Canadian woodsmen or of the conquest of Mexico, the adventures of the African folk, all add a dimension to cultural understanding when the teacher-storyteller draws from the wealth of material that social studies present.

Regional America, too, is rich in background for stories in the oral tradition. Tales from the coasts of New England, the plantations of the Old South, the forests and trails of the North, the rolling plains of the Midwest, the cattle country of the Southwest and the gleaming mountains and waters of the Far West all promise to reveal the flavor of the region from which they have come. The study of our own United States could be an exciting, fruitful adventure in learning if the teacher is a storyteller too. What exciting units could be developed if the history and geography of the United States were to be studied through its folk and oral tradition.

One of the richest sources in the social studies for the teacher-storyteller is the folk history of the community in which he lives. With the rapid growth of many communities and the projected growth that is likely to continue in the next decade, the folk roots of an area are likely to be forgotten, or at best, neglected. What a delight it is for a child to know the meaning of his town's name and how it came to be called by that name. How exciting it is to learn that a covered wagon stop once was where the supermarket stands today. What thrilling tales can derive from the events of the early settlers of the community and how they started the town that exists today. Wonderful tales exist in every community.

Really exciting tales do not always come from major events. That a community was once a stopping point for the Pony Express, or a fueling place for river boats, or a meeting ground for traders and Indians, any such historical fact is enough to start the storyteller off on rich adventures with his listeners. These events are unique and belong to the community. They are the tales that can be told and retold with special meaning in their own special setting. This is cultural heritage being handed down by the storyteller in the true folk tradition.

Stories to undergird the social studies and other curriculum areas all need the same preparation as do the old tales that were outlined earlier in this book. Most of them fall into the melodramatic structure and lend themselves to preparation as discussed earlier. If the structure changes, this should not deter the storyteller. The skeletal outline of incidents is still necessary to preserve the story for telling. A collection of tales to enhance the social studies would be a most useful part of any teacher-storyteller's repertoire.

Other Curriculum Areas

As in social studies, many other curricular areas can be enhanced by the art of storytelling. The lives of famous scientists and how they worked toward the great discoveries they made, or stories of their childhood, can bring a dimension that is often lacking in many elementary science programs. Stories about the great composers and artists can bring to children a personal involvement with these masters, an involvement that can add readiness to learn and additional understanding to children's interaction with their work. Here are great dramas with real opportunities to gain valuable insights, as well as additional and worthwhile information.

Stories about the holidays are special delights for the storyteller and his audience. These tales add a valuable dimension of cultural heritage. Be the holidays regional or national, religious or cultural manifestations, the stories they can provide will give hours of delight and learning. There are many handsome volumes ready and waiting to be utilized by the teacher who tells stories. Among the many available, these four seem to be favorites of teacher-storytellers:

EPSTEIN, SAM and BERYLE. *Spring Holidays.* Scarsdale, N.Y.: Garrard Publishing Co., 1964.

GUILFOILE, ELIZABETH. *Valentine's Day.* Scarsdale, N.Y.: Garrard Publishing Co., 1965.

JOHNSON, LOIS S., ed. *Christmas Stories Around the World.* Chicago: Rand McNally & Co., 1960.

UNWIN, NORA S. *Two Too Many.* New York: David McKay Co., Inc., 1962.

Aperture Limited of California, Inc., Stockton, California   John Adams Elementary School, Stockton, California

Books are seen in a special way after a storyteller tells a tale. The ancient art of storytelling often adds a new dimension to children's reaction to literature.

The storyteller's art undergirding areas of the curriculum can and will provide an extra dimension to the teaching process. It can take many disciplines from the realm of the often dreary textbook and raise them to great heights of exciting, fruitful experiences in learning. Storytelling as a pedagogical technique has been used by the world's greatest teachers. Jesus used it, as did Plato, Confucius, and other great philosophers and teachers. It is an instructional technique that did not belong only in the past. It has relevance to today's teacher, as well. The modern teacher who employs this technique as a teaching tool is using an ancient method that is as modern as tomorrow. That teacher is using a technique of teaching that has stood the test of time.

Points for Discussion and Things To Do

1. Examine a social studies unit. How would the storyteller's art enhance that unit?

2. Choose an incident from a social studies or history textbook, or a folktale that is related to a social studies unit. Prepare it for telling and then tell it.
3. Prepare a story for telling about a famous person in history (or science, art, etc.). Tell the story and note the reaction of the listeners to this personage's work and contributions to society.
4. Examine a collection of folktales from a foreign land. What insights into the culture of that land do you find?
5. Read some regional tales of the United States. Discuss how these tales reflect the "flavor" of the various areas.

selected references

The development of an adequate bibliography in any area is a long and difficult job. To develop one in an area such as storytelling, when the entire world of literature is open to consideration, is a monumental task. A bibliography is necessary, however, as a place for the beginning storyteller to start. The following bibliography is a limited one, restricted to sources that the writer feels will give momentum to the collecting of stories good for telling. It is designed to start the teacher-storyteller on what it is hoped will be a delightful treasure hunt through the realms of literature.

The writer has been arbitrary in categorizing the entries. Much discussion could be generated as to whether a collection of stories belongs under Regional Stories from the United States or under Tales to Enhance the Curriculum. Do Myths, Fairy Tales, and General Tales really belong under Foreign Tales? If discussion and disagreement should result, the writer would be delighted. Disagreement means activity, and activity could mean a revival of this special art.

On Telling:

CALLWELL, EILEEN. *A Second Storyteller's Choice.* New York: Henry Z. Walck, Inc., 1965.

CUNDIFF, RUBY ETHEL, and WEBB, BARBARA. *Storytelling for You: Handbook of Help for Storytellers Everywhere.* Yellow Springs, Ohio: Antioch Press, 1957.

SAWYER, RUTH. *The Way of the Storyteller.* New York: The Viking Press, Inc., 1962.

SHEDLOCK, MARIE L. *The Art of the Storyteller.* New York: Dover Publications, Inc., 1951.

TOOZE, RUTH. *Storytelling.* Englewood Cliffs, N. J.: Prentice-Hall, Inc., 1959.

Myths, Fairy Tales, and General Tales Good for Telling:

ALEXANDER, BEATRICE. *Famous Myths of the Golden Age*. New York: Random House, Inc., 1947.

ANDERSEN, HANS C. *It's Perfectly True and Other Stories*. Translated by Paul Levssac. New York: Harcourt, Brace & World, Inc., 1938.

ARBUTHNOT, MAY HILL. *Time for Fairy Tales Old and New*. Chicago: Scott, Foresman & Company, 1952.

ASBJÖRNSEN, PETER C. *East O' the Sun and West O' the Moon*. Garden City, N. J.: Junior Deluxe Editions, 1952.

CHILD STUDY ASSOCIATION OF AMERICA. *Holiday Storybook*. New York: Crowell, 1942.

COMMAGER, HENRY STEELE. *The St. Nicholas Anthology*. New York: Random House, Inc., 1948.

GÁG, WANDA. *Tales from Grimm*. New York: Coward-McCann, Inc., 1936.

GREEN, ROGER. *Once upon a Time*. New York: The Golden Press, Inc., 1962.

HUBER, MIRIAM BLANTON. *Story and Verse for Children*. New York: The Macmillan Company, 1955.

JACOBS, JOSEPH. *Celtic Fairy Tales*. New York: G. P. Putnam's Sons, n.d. (Many collections of fairy tales by Jacobs are available.)

JOHNSON, EDNA et al. *Anthology of Children's Literature*. Boston: Houghton Mifflin Company, 1959.

LANG, ANDREW. *The Blue Fairy Book*. New York: David McKay Co., Inc., 1948. (Many fine collections by Lang available.)

OPCOTT, FRANCES J. *Good Stories for Great Holidays*. Boston: Houghton Mifflin Company, 1941.

PERRAULT, CHARLES. *Perrault's Complete Fairy Tales*. New York: Dodd, Mead & Co., 1961.

UNTERMEYER, BRYNA and LOUIS. *World's Great Stories*. New York: M. Evans & Co., Inc., 1964.

———. *Fun and Fancy*. New York: The Golden Press, Inc., 1958.

———. *Legendary Animals*. New York: The Golden Press, Inc., 1954.

WATSON, KATHERINE W. *Tales for Telling*. New York: H. W. Wilson, Co., 1950.

Regional Stories from the United States:

BLAIR, WALTER. *Tall Tale America*. New York: Coward-McCann, Inc., 1944.

BOATRIGHT, BODY C., ed. *The Sky Is My Tipi*. The Texas Folklore Society. Dallas: University Press, 1949.

BOWMAN, JAMES C. *Pecos Bill: The Greatest Cowboy of All Time*. Chicago: Albert Whitman & Co., 1959. (Also, *The Adventures of Paul Bunyan*, etc. available through this publisher.)

CALIFORNIA HISTORY FOUNDATION. *The Pacific Historian*, a quarterly magazine. Stockton, Calif.: University of the Pacific Press, 1966.

CHASE, RICHARD. *The Grandfather Tales*. Boston: Houghton Mifflin Company, 1948.

———. *The Jack Tales*. Boston: Houghton Mifflin Company, 1960.

DOBIE, CHARLES CALDWELL. *San Francisco Tales*. New York: Appleton-Century-Crofts, 1938.

EMBERLEY, BARBARA. *The Story of Paul Bunyan.* Englewood Cliffs, N. J.: Prentice-Hall, Inc., 1963.

FIELD, RACHEL. *American Folk and Fairy Tales.* New York: Charles Scribner's Sons, 1929.

FISHER, ANNE B. *Stories California Indians Told.* Berkeley: Parnassus Press, 1957.

HAYNES, BESSIE D., and EDGAR. *The Grizzly Bear: Portraits from Life.* Norman: University of Oklahoma Press, 1966.

HICKOK, PEGGY. *Favorite Hawaiian Legends.* Honolulu: Tongg Publishing Co., 1961.

LEACH, MARIA. *The Rainbow Book of American Folktales and Legends.* Cleveland: World Publishing Company, 1958.

PITCHFORD, GENIE. *Young Folks Hawaiian Time.* Honolulu: Watkins and Sturgis, Ltd., 1964.

SACKETT, S. F., and KOCH, WILLIAM E. *Kansas Folklore.* Lincoln: University of Nebraska Press, 1961.

SHAPIRO, IRWIN. *Tall Tales of America.* Poughkeepsie: Guild Press, Inc., 1959.

SNEDDEN, CENEVA S. *Docas Indian of Santa Clara.* Boston: D. C. Heath & Company, 1958.

Foreign Tales Good for Telling:

ARNOTT, KATHLEEN. *African Myths and Legends.* New York: Henry Z. Walck, Inc., 1963.

BUCK, PEARL, ed. *Fairy Tales of the Orient.* New York: Simon and Schuster, Inc., 1965.

CARPENTER, FRANCES. *Tales of a Korean Grandmother.* Garden City, N. Y.: Doubleday & Company, Inc., 1947. (Carpenter has many such volumes of stories including Basque, Russian, Chinese, and Swiss.)

COURLANDER, HAROLD. *Terrapin's Pot of Sense.* New York: Holt, 1957. (Many other good volumes by Courlander.)

FINGER, CHARLES F. *Tales from Silver Lands.* Garden City, N.Y.: Doubleday & Company, Inc., 1924.

HENIUS, FRANK. *Stories from the Americas.* New York: Charles Scribner's Sons, 1944.

LORIMER, E. O., ed. *Tales from the Arabian Nights.* New York: Henry Z. Walck, Inc., 1962.

OBLIGADO, GEORGE, trans. *The Magic Butterfly and Other Fairy Tales of Central Europe.* New York: The Golden Press, Inc., 1963.

———. *The Warrior and the Princess, and Other South American Fairy Tales.* New York: The Golden Press, Inc., 1961.

PITT, GIORANDO. *Scandinavian Fairy Tales.* New York: The Golden Press, Inc., 1962.

———, trans. *Russian Fairy Tales.* New York: The Golden Press, Inc., 1960.

PONSOT, MARIE. *Tales of India, Selected from the Mahabharata.* New York: The Golden Press, Inc., 1961.

REEVES, JAMES. *English Fables and Fairy Stories.* New York: Oxford University Press, Inc., 1955.

Tales to Enhance the Curriculum:

Coy, Harold. *The Americans.* Boston: Little, Brown and Company, 1958.

Daugherty, James. *Trappers and Traders of the Far West.* New York: Random House, Inc., 1952.

Gridley, Marion. *Indian Legends of American Scenes.* New York: M. A. Donohue & Co., 1939.

Judd, Gerrit P. *Hawaii, an Informal History.* New York: Collier Books, 1961.

Miers, Earl S. *The Rainbow Book of American History.* Cleveland: The World Publishing Company, 1955.

Rushmore, Helen and Hunt, Wolf Robe. *The Dancing Horses of Acoma.* New York: The World Publishing Company, 1963.

section

two

creative
drama

chapter 5

creative drama:
a natural part
of childhood

Pretending at play is a natural part of childhood. Youngsters in all countries and cultures, history tells us, have spent much of their leisure play time pretending to be characters and to have adventures that are imaginary. It is obvious to us when we watch today's children at their games that they, too, enjoy pretending. The rowdy "Cowboys and Indians," "Cops and Robbers," or "Pirates" and other favorite characterizations of the young boy all give evidence of this need to pretend at play. The more gentle "dolls," "playing house," or "going to market" that are favorites of girls, likewise are manifestations of this need to utilize imaginative drama as a part of play activity.

Some writers have suggested that play activity of this nature (when the child pretends an adult role) is really preparatory education for life as an adult.[1] They suggest that children, through their imaginative play, try on the cloak and role of the adult so that they will be better able to cope with the realities and duties of the adult when they reach maturity. It is a theory that offers some food for thought.

Certainly, when we watch young animals at play, we are inclined to believe that this is true. The puppy plays at combat and the hunt. The kitten spends much of her time playing at stalking, pouncing, and practicing the lightning-like paw movements that will put her in good stead when she becomes a cat. These baby animals, like their human counterparts, are perhaps answering an ancient instinct to pretend activities that they will need in later years. Perhaps these games of the young are a rehearsal for the drama of later life.

This need to create drama in play has been understood and valued by the toy industry for many years. If one were to walk through a toy

[1]Erik Erikson, *Insight and Responsibility* (New York: W. W. Norton & Company, Inc., 1964).

store or through the toy section of a department store, he would find definite proof of this. There is a dazzling variety of material available to the child so that he can meet this need to pretend at play. Much of this material is geared to the kind of imaginative, dramatic play that would, as some suggest, permit the youngster to prepare for his adult role. Dolls, miniature home appliances, make-believe weapons, costumes depicting various adult occupations, mock technical tools, etc. await the child, or the adult buyer. The monetary return from the manufacture and sale of this material is staggering. Industrial giants are literally created by this catering to the play needs of children.

The teacher who knows about this play need that children have, and utilizes it in his educational scheme, is a wise teacher indeed. The educational possibilities of an activity of this nature are seemingly endless. The teacher who knows the values and techniques of creative drama brings into his classroom one of the most flexible and creative tools available to the professional educator.

Creative drama is a form of pretending at play. It is a structured play experience that is carefully planned and executed. With creative drama, children create or re-create a scene, an episode, a problem, or an event, usually from children's literature, under teacher guidance. The play activity is discussed and planned by the children and is also evaluated by them. Dramatic technique is involved in the execution of a creative drama in that children are creating and playing roles, but the activity cannot be termed "drama" in the traditional sense. Scripts are never used. Costumes are most often unnecessary. Properties and scenery play no part in an activity of this kind. The performance of a creative drama is viewed not from the point of view of a possible audience, but of the participants themselves. The final product is not the major issue in creative drama, although it is important that it needs to be satisfying. The process involved with a creative drama is the issue. The process of creating the structured play is the central core of this activity, and from the process, the learning emerges.

Creative drama should not be confused with dramatic play or with other activities that employ drama as a factor in execution. Dramatic play is most often spontaneous, unstructured . . . free dramatic activity. Playing with toy trucks or pretending to drive one of them would be dramatic play activity. The free play of kindergarten children in the playhouse is likewise often dramatic play, as would be "Cowboys and Indians" and "Cops and Robbers" on the playground. Creative drama demands structure, planning, and evaluation. Dramatic play does not.

Certainly, creative drama should not be confused with theatre for children or theatre with children. It is not playmaking in the theatrical sense at all.

⋆Likewise, creative drama should not be confused with role-playing or socio-drama. These latter two techniques, though they are similar in preparation and execution, are quite unlike creative drama in their purpose. Role-playing and socio-drama have overtones of psychological therapy involved in them. Creative drama is not a therapeutic technique, nor should it be used as such.

✝Creative drama is a short, structured dramatic play activity, wherein the emphasis is placed on the process, rather than on the product. It should be spontaneous and creative; it should show depth of insight into the characters played and the issues involved; it should be free of formalized theatrics; and it should provide satisfaction, if not real delight, to those who involve themselves with it. It is a natural part of childhood which can easily and successfully be employed by teachers of elementary school students.

As Menagh wrote, "The requirements of creative dramatics are few, consisting only of a group of children with a qualified leader and a space in which to function. There is no need for a script or for the technical aids so frequently associated with theatre production . . . no scenery, lighting, costumes or make-up. The only physical environment required is a space such as almost any classroom can provide with the tables and chairs pushed back. These tables or desks and chairs may, of course be used from time to time. There is no audience but that possibly provided by the participants themselves. . ."[2]

The genesis for the most successful experiences with creative drama is found between the covers of good children's literature. The folktale, incidents from children's novels, short stories for children, etc. all offer real opportunities to engage in this very special kind of creative activity, an activity that can add a special dimension to the realm of children's literature.

"Books become more real to children as they identify with the characters through creative dramatics . . . children play out the story as they "believe" in the roles they assume. The teacher's major concern is with the process and values of the children involved . . . the value of creative drama lies in the process of playing. . ."[3]

---

[2]H. Beresford Menagh, "Creative Dramatics" in *Guiding Children's Language Learning*, Pose Lamb, ed. (Dubuque, Iowa: Wm. C. Brown Company Publishers, 1967), p. 63.
[3]Charlotte S. Huck and Doris Young Kuhn, *Children's Literature in the Elementary School*. 2d. ed. (New York: Holt, Rinehart & Winston, Inc., 1968), p. 625.

chapter 6

getting started with a new technique

Pretending at play is a natural part of being young. We see the need for this activity whenever we watch youngsters during their free playtime. Despite this, it is sometimes less than easy to start an activity of this nature in some classrooms. This is especially true of the middle grade classroom. The middle grade student often believes that an activity like creative drama doesn't belong in the classroom. It is "too much fun" to be of value. Some children are actually conditioned to think that learning should not be enjoyable. Also, they are sometimes shy, uncertain, and hesitant about the act of pretending in a structured situation with and before their peer group and their teacher. The less inhibited primary age youngster seems much more able to interact immediately with this technique, than does the middle grade child. This is probably so because the younger child has not developed as far socially as has his older counterpart, and is thus less concerned with peer and teacher opinion.

Even with primary youngsters, the stage must be set, and children must be made to feel secure before a teacher can launch into a creative drama activity that will provide all the value that is inherent in the employment of this technique. Certainly, if youngsters have never experienced creative drama, a readiness program for this activity is a most important variable in its success. One simply cannot move into a creative drama session and provide a valuable experience with it unless children have had experience with the technique and feel free to use it in a classroom setting.

How does a teacher provide readiness for creative drama? What activities can lead up to a successful experience with creative drama? How can a teacher help provide for children the feeling of security and ease that is needed to create a drama? Certainly, the classroom variables that are discussed on page 71 of this book are most important. The emotional climate of a classroom is probably the most important ingredient in this creative endeavor.

If the classroom climate provides an environment that is rich with children's literature, safe, relaxed, purposeful, and conducive to creative expression, the teacher can then provide readiness activity for creative drama. Some of the most successful readiness activities are:

1. CHARADE.   Charade is a guessing game that is popular with adults. In Charade, words or titles are acted out syllable by syllable until the word or title is guessed. It is an involved game and takes real skill to play it well. In its pure form, it is not suitable for most children. A modified charade is a good game for children and an excellent lead-up to creative drama.

   In a charade for children, teams are formed, often by splitting the class in half. In the game, each team is numbered from one to fifteen, more or less, depending upon the size of the class, each youngster receiving a number. The number he receives indicates the order in which he will play the charade, or act out the word or title for his team to guess. The player is allowed a specified length of time (usually two minutes) to act out his word or title. During this time, he may not speak. He must act out the word or title silently, the while encouraging or discouraging the responses from his team by gesture or silent activity. If, at the end of his allotted time, his team hasn't correctly guessed his charade, he must return to his seat. If the team guesses his charade, his team makes one point. At the end of his allotted time, whether or not his team has guessed his charade, the activity goes to the opposing team. They in turn attempt to earn a point in the same manner. The title is given orally by the teacher who also serves as time-keeper, score-keeper, and umpire.

   Usually a box of words or titles is kept for Charade. Titles of children's books, television programs that children watch, motion picture titles, etc. supply the material for the guessing game. Many teachers ask children to supply words and titles to go into the *Charade Box*. Others supply words for the box themselves. It is important that the words and titles that go into the *Charade Box* are not esoteric. They should be words and titles that are known by all the children.

   When the game starts, player number one of team number one reaches into the *Charade Box* and draws a word or title. He reads it and then hands it to the teacher who puts it to one side. He takes his allotted time to act out the word or title for his team to guess. Team number two moves in the same way. The team that has the most points at the end of the game wins.

This game is fun, and team spirit often makes it highly competitive. Youngsters, in their attempt to help their team members guess their words or titles, will use the imagery, the action, and the activity so necessary for a good creative drama. It is usually easier for children to pretend in creative drama after they have played Charade several times.

2. CAN YOU GUESS? This activity is somewhat like Charade, but lacks the team element, and thus the competition. It also demands more imagery and more ability to pretend than does Charade. It is an excellent lead-up to creative drama.

On a table or desk that is centrally located and easily seen by all class members, an imaginary box is placed. No one knows how large this imaginary box is, or how it is wrapped, or what it contains. Finding what it contains is the game.

Children volunteer to come to the desk and "open" this imaginary box. It is their job to show the class how large it is, if it is wrapped in a special way, and what it contains. Children and teacher watch until the youngster has completed his activity with the imaginary box. Then they try to guess what was in it. The one who guesses correctly gets the next turn to work with the imaginary box.

It is good if the teacher involves herself several times with the imaginary box. If she does so, and children see that this pretending has her interest too, the activity will move with greater speed. It is always delightful to watch children during this activity. The creative, and often ingenious, way in which youngsters play this game gives valuable, and sometimes surprising, insights into their abilities and personalities.

3. HOW DO I FEEL? This game, much like "Can You Guess?", also operates as a guessing game without team competition. In this activity, the youngster walks into the room from the outside and affects an attitude that reveals how he "feels." He may be tired, warm, angry, gay, sad, hungry, etc. Once he has taken a place at the front of the room, the children try to guess "how he feels." The one who guesses correctly has the next turn to show how he "feels."

There are many variations to this kind of guessing game. Such activities as DO YOU BELIEVE ME?, HOW DOES IT LOOK?, WHAT'S WRONG?, all offer real possibilities for children to learn the skills of imagery. The creative teacher will devise other games and activities that will help to provide the same skills.

Games of this type are designed to help children feel at ease with creative drama in the classroom. It is usually a simple matter to move from these games of imagery into creative drama.

The First Session with Creative Drama

The first creative drama session that children have is a most important one. It will likely set the pace for those that follow. It is important that the teacher so structure this first drama that success with it is almost automatic and guaranteed.

The first creative drama should be a short, uncomplicated one. It should contain few characters and few incidents. The more sophisticated and advanced dramas can come later. For the first, however, simplicity is the order. Children with their first drama sometimes become nervous and confused. The teacher needs to plan for this possibility. Planning a simple scene is a wise practice. For example, without using dialogue, a child might portray Cinderella's flight from the ball at midnight; Snow White's stepmother's confrontation with the mirror; Rip Van Winkle's return to civilization; a scene from Pinnochio; or any other simple scene from a generally known story.

Children need to be aware of the steps necessary in building creative drama (see chapter 8). The wise teacher knows the importance of explaining what these steps are and of emphasizing each step as she and the youngsters proceed with their first drama. This emphasis on the process will pay dividends later on. The teacher wants her children to understand the steps in creative drama so well that they can, in time, move from one step to the next easily and almost automatically.

When it is time to choose players for the first scene, the teacher would be wise to select youngsters who she knows will do well. This may seem dishonest and perhaps a little as though the teacher is manipulating children, but the reverse is really true. The first drama needs as many safeguards as possible to insure success. This first drama will serve as an example; it will be the cornerstone upon which future dramas are built. Its success is very important. Picking the first cast with this in mind is simply good technique in group dynamics. When a good example of creative drama is presented in the first one, and children are facile with the technique, a wider casting practice can be applied. The first cast, however, needs to be selected with care so that success is highly probable.

Some successful leaders of creative drama believe that the teacher should be involved in the children's first experience with the technique. This may be a good idea, depending upon the makeup of the group and the ability of the teacher. If the teacher, however, feels uneasy about involving herself in a creative drama, it is best that she keep out of it. On the other hand, there is little question as to the value of the teacher's involvement in the first drama if she feels comfortable about doing a role. Her involvement will offer additional stability to the playing and give "official acceptance" to the technique as being a part of the classroom operation.

As with any new approach, new technique, or new experience with children, the teacher moves slowly and carefully at first. Readiness for, and success with, the first experience in any technique is simply good teaching. This kind of good teaching is essential to success with creative drama. Once an initial successful experience has been achieved with creative drama in any classroom, one of the most exciting, creative approaches to good learning is readily available.

Points for Discussion and Things To Do

1. Discuss, in depth, why primary children may be, or frequently appear to be, more at ease with creative drama than are middle grade children.
2. Organize a game of Charade in your classroom. If your classroom is at the college level, play Charade as an adult game first, then as a children's game. Use titles of children's books for your charades.
3. What other games of imagery can you devise that will serve as good readiness activities for creative drama? Play them in your classroom.
4. Are all stories good for middle grade creative drama? Are all stories good for primary grade creative drama? What qualities should you seek in stories for each group?
5. What stories, and specifically what scenes in them, would be good for a first experience with creative drama?
6. Discuss qualities you will look for in children when you cast the parts in the following scenes from children's books:
   a. Fern's reaction to her father's disenchantment with Wilbur, in E. B. White's *Charlotte's Web*.
   b. Tom and the boys in the white-washing sequence, in Mark Twain's *Tom Sawyer*.
   c. The court jester's conversation with Princess Lenore when he finds out that there is more than one moon, in James Thurber's *Many Moons*.
   d. The Troll's encounter with the largest of the goats, in Grimms' *The Billy Goats Gruff*.
   e. Aladdin's reaction to the magic of his lamp when he discovers it for the first time, in Andrew Lang's *Arabian Nights*.

f. The stepmother and two stepsisters, the Prince, and Cinderella in the scene where Cinderella reveals that she was the Princess at the ball, in Perrault's *Cinderella*.

g. Rumpelstiltskin's reaction to the Queen when she finally guesses his name, in Grimms' *Rumpelstiltskin*.

7. What is your feeling about involving yourself, as a teacher, in a creative drama session? How do you account for these feelings?

8. Discuss why a successful first experience with creative drama is important.

chapter 7

creative drama
in action

All thirty-three youngsters in Mr. William Miller's fourth grade class leaned forward so as not to miss one word. Mr. Miller was telling a story, and the probability of creative drama developing from that story was obvious if one knew the climate and operating procedure of that class. An observer could see that the children were experiencing enjoyment. One could sense, also, the anticipation of the activity that would follow the telling of the story. The children fully expected to "pretend" all or parts of that delightful old French tale, *Stone Soup*[1] that Mr. Miller was telling.

The story rollicked along as the three hungry, poverty-stricken French soldiers approached the village with plans to bilk the villagers into preparing a banquet which would start with the boiling of the "magic" stone in a large kettle of water. The children smiled broadly when the leader of the three soldiers, after tasting the boiling water and extolling its flavor, mentioned how much better the magic soup would be if only some onions, carrots, potatoes, meat, barley, etc. could be added. The youngsters shook their heads in mock disbelief as the villagers, one by one, brought the ingredients to the soldiers to be added to the stone soup so as to make it "the finest soup in all of France."

The children laughed heartily as the leader of the soldiers further convinced the gullible villagers that a soup as fine as this one really needed a banquet to go along with it. Their enjoyment increased as Mr. Miller told of the fine fare that came from the villagers' kitchens to the square where the magic soup was bubbling in the kettle. Ham, roast beef, chicken, fruits, wine and milk, pies, cakes, tarts, and other delicious foods to make a feast fit for "the King himself" found their way to the

---

[1]Marcia Brown, *Stone Soup* (New York: Charles Scribner's Sons, 1947).

soldiers who were exclaiming about the wonders of the soup their "magic" stone had created.

The tale continued as the soldiers sat with the mayor and other dignitaries at the head of a large table and enjoyed the great feast that their "magic" stone had prompted. The children relished the fact that the soldiers had completely fooled the villagers, but they also realized that the villagers had really expected to receive something for nothing and had had the tables turned on them.

Whoops of laughter greeted the part of the tale where the soldiers presented the mayor with the magic stone, and he in turn promised to make a monument for it so that all the people of France could come and admire the wonderful stone that could produce a banquet.

Mr. Miller ended his telling of *Stone Soup* by saying that he had been told that somewhere in France, even today, that monument to a "magic" stone stands. He said he didn't know where it was . . . in fact, he indicated with a twinkle in his eye, that he wondered if it really existed . . . or ever did.

The children were thrilled and most satisfied when Mr. Miller finished his telling of *Stone Soup*. He was a good storyteller, and he told his tale with skill. The youngsters knew his prowess with the art of storytelling and were once again reinforced with a feeling that they were fortunate indeed to have a teacher with that skill and ability.

As soon as Mr. Miller finished the story, hands shot into the air and requests to "pretend" *Stone Soup* poured forth. Mr. Miller and the class had obviously had many experiences with creative drama, but had named the technique "Pretending." It seems that the semantics of "Pretending" outweighed the more formal term "creative drama," at least in the minds of these fourth graders. "Pretending," at least, is what they wanted to do now that the tale had been told.

Mr. Miller readily agreed that it would be a good idea to pretend *Stone Soup*. He and the class then started the preparations for the experience.

Together, the teacher and the pupils reconstructed the story. Mr. Miller, at the chalkboard, listened to the youngsters as they constructed the tale, incident by incident, or as they termed it, "scene by scene." As they dictated, he noted the incidents on the board:

1. The three soldiers tell about their problem and see the village in the distance.
2. The soldiers make plans to fool the people.
3. The soldiers go into the square and get the attention of the people. They tell about the "magic" stone and how it can make soup.
4. The villagers are fooled. They provide a kettle, a fire, and some water. The soldiers boil the stone, but get the villagers to bring other things for the soup.

Aperture Limited of California, Inc., Stockton,   John Adams Elementary School, Stockton, Cali-
California   fornia

Any successful experience with creative drama demands preparation.
Students and teacher need to plan carefully what they will do and how
they will do it.

5. The soldiers and the villagers hold a banquet to go along with the
   soup.
6. The soldiers say farewell and leave the "magic" stone with the mayor.
   He will build a monument to the stone.

Some may argue that the reconstruction of the plot of *Stone Soup*,
as outlined above, is incomplete and oversimplified. For a group of fourth
graders, however, (and they led the discussion) it represented a high level
of group thinking. From their point of view, the incidents listed on the
chalkboard represented the sequence of the tale and the high points
of the story. They were incidents, the youngsters felt, that could be
"pretended," and if done in sequence, would tell the story of *Stone Soup*
to their satisfaction.

Mr. Miller reviewed the sequence again with the children. He read directly from their dictated outline on the chalkboard. What scenes, he asked, would the class like to pretend? To do the entire story would be lengthy, and time is always a problem in any classroom.

The children discussed what they thought would be best and concluded that scenes 3 and 4 would be the ones that they would "pretend." Mr. Miller erased the other scenes, leaving only those two:

3. The soldiers go into the square and get the attention of the people. They tell about the "magic" stone and how it can make soup.
4. The villagers are fooled. They provide a kettle, a fire, and some water. The soldiers boil the stone, but get the villagers to bring other things for the soup.

Now that the story had been defined in sequence, and two sequences or "scenes" had been chosen as the ones to pretend, the preparation for the "pretending" itself began.

Mr. Miller again initiated and led the discussion. This time, the youngsters broke the two chosen scenes down into further incidents. Mr. Miller's prodding questions such as "What happened first?", "Then what happened?", "What happened next?" helped the children clarify the structure of the two sequences. At the end of that discussion, the children knew very well how the scenes, in terms of plot line, would be played.

The discussion then turned to an analysis of the characters. Under Mr. Miller's guidance, the pupils analyzed reasons for the soldiers doing what they did. Such issues as these were considered: Were they evil men? Why weren't they with the rest of the army? Were they clever? Were they all equally clever? How were they able to convince the villagers that the stone could make soup, and what does this tell us about these soldiers? Did the soldiers hurt anyone? Have any of us ever tried to fool someone?

Next, the discussion turned to the soldiers' physical appearance. The youngsters created the soldiers physically . . . they dressed them, they determined their degree of hunger and fatigue, they defined their physical properties of weight and height, they described each in terms of facial characteristics and personality type. Mr. Miller made available a copy of Marcia Brown's *Stone Soup*. It served as the final authority on the physical appearance of the soldiers and the villagers. A well-illustrated version of a story that is being prepared for creative drama is always a helpful reference, especially if the manner of dress and the physical settings are foreign to children.

The youngsters then, along with Mr. Miller, described the setting. They talked about the buildings, the square, the general appearance of the village. They designated the spot where the soldiers would make their plea, and the place where the kettle would sit for the action that followed. It would be a simple matter to push desks back to make room for the setting that had been described.

As the discussion continued, the youngsters and the teacher wove the warp and woof of the fabric of literary analysis. The setting, the main characters, their motivations, their physical make-up, and their personalities all became clear to the children as they discussed and planned for this session of creative drama. Not all the children saw the characters or the setting in the same way. Some openly disagreed with the interpretation of another. And yet, the characters of *Stone Soup* took on an extra dimension, a physical life, an exciting reality that few literary heroes ever achieve.

Next, the villagers came under scrutiny. Why did they believe the soldiers? How did they feel when the soldiers first came into the village? How did they feel when the soup started to boil? What kind of people were they? Have any of us ever been fooled? Why were you able to be fooled? Do you think the villagers wanted to be fooled? Questions and ideas flashed about the classroom like a mock electric storm.

The number of villagers to be in the scene and what each was to contribute to the soup were determined.

The structure of the creative drama had been built. Sequence of events had been established. Motivations had been understood. Characterization had been defined. The planning session was coming to an end.

Choosing of the characters was not an easy matter. Hands shot into the air as the pupils sought to request certain roles. Two boys and a girl were finally selected by Mr. Miller to play the soldiers. That a girl was to play a soldier didn't matter at all. After all, this was pretend! Ten villagers were chosen in the same way, and each defined what he would bring to the soup.

The children who were to play the characters removed themselves from the main classroom group, and at Mr. Miller's request, planned together more exactly how they would play the scenes. They were limited to about five minutes for group planning. From the concentration they evidenced at their meeting, they weren't about to waste any time.

While this was going on, Mr. Miller had turned his attention to the remainder of the class. He had them move desks and chairs back so that a playing area was made available in the front of the room. He then asked the children to watch the "Pretend" so that they could evaluate the session and perhaps make it better when it was played again with a new set of players. He reminded them that during the second or third "Pretend," any one of them watching now could be playing roles later. The children seemed to understand this very well and appeared to be very serious as to how the scenes would be played. There was no nonsense, no childish misbehavior. They were deeply interested and personally involved in the results of this session. Mr. Miller gave one final direction to the audience. He asked them to watch the "Pretend" for five things they liked about it, and five things they would change if they were to play the scene. It was evident that Mr. Miller was interested in helping these children learn that criticism can be valuable if it is positive criticism as well as negative.

Mr. Miller asked the players if they were ready to start. They answered, somewhat reluctantly, that they "thought so". . . but could use more time to plan. Mr. Miller good-naturedly urged them to start their "Pretend," and when they had settled into their predetermined stations, he signaled that the "Pretend" would begin.

Three tired, hungry soldiers walked to the center of the playing area. They limped and were very bedraggled. But under the urging of the leader, they stopped in the middle of the village square and tried to present a very striking picture. The villagers all watched the soldiers with interest, suspicion, and a great deal of whispering.

The leader of the three soldiers called for the attention of the villagers. He urged them to step forward and receive some "special news." At the prodding of the three soldiers, the villagers surged forward and prepared to listen.

From his pocket, the leader withdrew an imaginary stone. He explained its magic qualities, and his claims were readily and audibly supported by the other soldiers. The leader told the villagers that the three of them were prepared to demonstrate the magic quality of the stone, but that they would need cooperation from them, the villagers. He indicated that he would need only a kettle filled with water, a fire, and a large spoon to stir the magic soup.

The villagers decided that they had "nothing to lose," and so several of them scurried "home" and brought "back" an imaginary kettle (two youngsters had to "carry" it), buckets of water, and wood for the fire. A large spoon was supplied from the imaginary kitchen of a village housewife.

The soldiers "lit" the fire, and with great ceremony, dropped the stone into the water. The lead soldier cautioned the villagers not to get too close, lest they get splashed. Besides, if they got too close, the magic might not work.

The soldiers, one by one, stirred the soup in the imaginary kettle. They sniffed it and exclaimed at the aroma. The villagers tried to get closer to see the magic take place but were cautioned to keep their distance.

Finally, the leader tasted the soup. He closed his eyes ecstatically and hummed his approval. Then he wrinkled his forehead and tasted it again. He indicated to his partners that "something seemed to be missing." It was a great soup, but "something just seemed to be missing." All tasted the soup and agreed that "something was indeed missing," something that could make the soup into a truly delicious food.

The villagers strained forward to hear the conversation among the soldiers. Several of them whispered among themselves that "something was missing" in the soup.

At last, the leader of the three soldiers spoke loudly and purposefully to his partners, declaring that the missing ingredient was meat. If only they had some meat to add to the soup, it would be a great soup. The two soldiers agreed readily, and the three of them talked loudly about needing meat for the soup . . . in order to make it a delicious soup, a soup "fit for the King himself."

Aperture Limited of California, Inc., Stockton,   John Adams Elementary School, Stockton, California
California   fornia

Creative drama in action. The characters of children's literature are brought to life when children pretend at play. Here the French soldiers confront villagers as they do in the story, **Stone Soup.**

One of the villagers spoke up and announced that he would bring some meat for the soup. He had pounds of it at home and would contribute it to the soup so that it would be "fit for the King himself."

He left the square and returned promptly with a large "basket of meat" and gave it to the soldiers. The soldiers thanked him most profusely and added the meat to the soup.

Again they stirred, sniffed, and tasted. Each time they did so, they found the soup to be "nearly perfect." And each time, they also found that the soup needed something extra . . . potatoes, onions, carrots, salt and pepper, tomatoes, and other ingredients. Each time they discovered "what was missing," an eager villager would rush to bring it to them from her kitchen. And so it went, the soldiers "creating" a wonderful soup with their "magic stone" and the villagers crowding around, curious and gullible.

At a nod from Mr. Miller, the "Pretend" ended. The soldiers and villagers stopped the soup-making and once again became fourth graders. They were obviously delighted with what they had done, and returned to the seating area amid showers of applause. Everyone seemed to be very happy about the entire experience. Mr. Miller congratulated the youngsters on a fine "Pretend." He told them that he really *believed* certain parts of the play. His use of the term "believed" indicated that the action had been very realistic and that it had been easy to understand and to follow. It was taken as a fine compliment.

When the players were seated and the momentary excitement subsided, Mr. Miller again directed the discussion. He reminded the class that they had been told to find five things they liked about the "Pretend," and five things they thought could be improved upon when it was played again.

The children were willing and eager to offer criticism of the session. Hands were raised and critical opinions were shared.

"I liked the way the soldiers limped when they came to the village. They looked tired and hungry."

"Judy did a good job as the middle soldier. I liked the way she agreed with the leader all the time."

"All the villagers were good. They really were fooled."

"I liked the way Bill stirred the soup. I could almost see that spoon in his hand."

"Bill really looked sly when he told the villagers he had a magic stone. I almost had to laugh."

"When John put the stone in the kettle of water, I liked the way the soldiers and the villagers jumped back so they wouldn't get splashed."

"I liked the way we could hear what they were saying. They spoke loudly and clearly."

Each youngster had indeed watched the "Pretend" with a critical eye. They had caught the nuances and subtle movements of the play and had enjoyed them. Their positive criticism was well given. They had much to praise and they did not stint in doing so. The children shared these criticisms with each other as naturally and as easily as they would have commented on a fine baseball team on the playground after school. Mr. Miller, also, pointed up what he thought had been especially fine pieces of playing.

When they had exhausted the areas of positive criticism, they turned to the areas that, according to them, needed improvement. The children offered suggestions and criticism of the play from this point of view just as easily as they had when they discussed the positive points.

"Bill needed to be more convincing when he talked to the villagers about the magic stone. He should have talked more . . . and faster if he was going to fool everyone. He should have been more like those guys who sell cars on TV."

"Alice and Betty giggled too much. The villagers wouldn't have done that."

"The other two soldiers just stood around too much. They should have done more. They left it all up to Bill."

"When Dick brought the onions in, it didn't look like he had enough of them. He just handed something to Bill."

"Charlie brought too many carrots. It looked like he was lugging a whole sack of them. I think he overdid it."

"I couldn't see how they lit the fire. They didn't wait long enough to let the water boil."

"Don didn't do anything."

And so it went. There seemed to be no malice, and several times, the players interrupted and explained what they had done and why they had done it. The discussion made it clear that, even though the "Pretend" was very good, it could be improved, and the weak areas were pointed out with amazing clarity.

Mr. Miller was always present to channel the negative criticism, so as not to let it disintegrate into an argument, or a personality assassination. He stepped in several times to soften what could have been a very harsh criticism.

After the discussion criticizing the play from both the positive and the negative aspects (it took about twelve minutes), the youngsters were ready to play the scenes again. This time, an entirely different group of children was selected to play the soldiers and the villagers. As before, the players moved to a corner of the room for a brief planning period, as Mr. Miller reviewed with the remaining students their responsibility during the "Pretend." They were of course to enjoy it, but they also were to watch it for five things they liked and five things they would improve if they were to play it again. Mr. Miller admitted that time might not permit playing the scenes a third time, as recess was scheduled and other classroom responsibilities had to be met. It would depend, however, on the amount of time they had left. One hour and fifteen minutes of class time was allotted for this activity.

At a signal, the new set of players replayed the scenes. The soldiers and villagers created the soup, and the scenes were completed. A rather different interpretation was evident in this playing. The characterizations of the soldiers were quite unlike those of the soldiers who had played before them. On the other hand, while the villagers had a reaction to the soldiers similar to that of the first set of villagers, individual characterizations were obvious. The criticism of the previous group certainly affected this "Pretend." The experience of the first group enhanced the second playing, and it was noticeably better.

When the playing had ended and the second group of players had returned to their seats, the discussion that followed proceeded along the same lines as did the discussion after the first "Pretend." The children criticized the play first from a positive point of view, then from a constructive point of view. The criticisms after the second playing had more depth and detail than did the first critical discussion. The children's perceptions were sharpened. They were able to see more, to evaluate more carefully. The simple French tale, *Stone Soup*, took on an entirely different dimension. It had been subjected to a kind of literary analysis that turned this plain little tale into an aesthetic experience of great value. If the children could transfer this kind of investigation to other pieces of their literature, their literary education was off to an impressive start.

Time did not permit a third playing. The room was put back in order, and the children went out to recess.

Mr. Miller and his fourth grade used *Stone Soup* as a genesis for their creative drama. It was an excellent choice. Many others of similar structure are equally fine, however. Such old favorites as *Rumpelstiltskin, Cinderella, Hansel and Gretel, The Shoemaker and the Elves, Tattercoats,* and *Sleeping Beauty* also offer good possibilities for creative drama. The folktale seems to be as much at home with creative drama as it is with the storyteller's art. For additional bibliography containing good tales to use with creative drama, see p. 73, and Selected References, p. 89.

chapter 8

an analysis
of creative
drama activity

One might well conclude, after reading the previous chapter, that Mr. Miller's fourth grade pupils had a rich background in creative drama. Few classes ever achieve that level of play the first time they engage in a creative drama activity. As a matter of fact, few classes achieve that level of play even after three or four attempts to "Pretend." Mr. Miller was experienced with this technique. His facility with creative drama activity, as well as his students' familiarity with it, had developed after several months' experience with the technique, producing the highly creative and valuable, from a literary standpoint, experience described in the foregoing pages.

It should not be concluded, however, that Mr. Miller was an exceptional teacher. He was a very fine, creative teacher who was willing to learn and to pass this learning on to his pupils in terms of new techniques and experiences, but he could hardly be termed "exceptional." His education was that of most teachers. He held a Bachelor's degree, and was working toward his Master's degree at a nearby university. Mr. Miller was a young man, just under thirty, and had a large amount of energy and boundless enthusiasm for his work. He was a highly competent professional but not necessarily exceptional.

The fourth grade class was not exceptional, either. It was as typical as any other fourth grade anywhere to be found. The pupils ranged in I.Q. and achievement from far below grade level to considerably above. Maturity level also had a wide span. Emotional problems, health problems, etc. were present in this fourth grade just as they are in most. The socio-economic level of the group was predominantly middle-class. It was a suburban group and was racially mixed. There was little that could be called exceptional about this group.

What happened in Mr. Miller's fourth grade can happen in most elementary school classrooms. The major variable in an experience such as the one described, is a teacher who is willing and able to learn about and to communicate the techniques of creative drama.

For the novice leader of creative drama, perhaps it would be well to analyze the experience of that fourth grade's creative drama activity. It might be well to examine the classroom variables and the steps taken to reach the level of competency that Mr. Miller's group reached. What is needed in a classroom setting? How does one go about turning the natural need to play that is in all children into a structured learning experience with literature?

The Classroom Climate

Any class that is expected to create and to engage in a creative drama activity needs to have a classroom climate that is conducive to such activity. That climate should be relaxed, safe, and flexible. It should permit experimentation and allow for mistakes. The classroom should be one in which children's comments and opinions are heard and valued.

The classroom in which effective creative drama activity occurs probably also would be one in which many kinds of creative activities take place. Creative art work, creative writing, construction activities, group projects, and the like, would always be evident. A rich literary environment, of course, would be a major variable.

"The classroom setting will allow for divergent learning patterns and will avoid the rigid syndrome that is so damaging to any learning, let alone learning of a creative nature. The classroom leader, the teacher, is familiar with and an exponent of creative teaching techniques that have, in recent years, become so important in modern classroom management."[1]

The classroom climate should reflect a mutual trust between pupils and teacher. The teacher should encourage pupil planning and evaluation of a learning experience as much as possible, for he will understand that his charges are imperfect young human beings who are in the process of growth and learning. It is important that the pupils know that their teacher values and appreciates them.

The classroom should exemplify order. The students will know that there are limitations to which the teacher expects them to adhere. There should be structure in the classroom, where the learning environment is carefully planned. The teacher should know that creativity and learning do not emerge from chaos. Real creativity and real learning come

---

[1]James A. Smith, *Setting Conditions for Creative Teaching in the Elementary School* (Boston: Allyn & Bacon, Inc., 1966).

Aperture Limited of California, Inc., Stockton, California

John Adams Elementary School, Stockton, California

For creative drama, as with any creative activity, classroom conditions need to be correct. A classroom with a safe, relaxed climate that encourages exploration is best. Children are then eager to create with drama.

from an orderly environment in which youngsters are purposefully engaged in work activity, rather than in disconnected, erratic behavior. The teacher should be a professional educational leader who has planned well and who knows his goals, in terms of educational objectives, and how to reach those goals. He should also know the importance of evaluation.

Creative drama, like any creative activity, needs a proper environment before it can grow and flourish. That environment must be provided or children will hesitate, and perhaps even refuse, to become engaged in anything so personally involving. If the proper environment is provided, however, creative dramatic activity can and will grow into a natural manifestation of good learning.

Stages of Development in Creative Drama

When one carefully examines the creative drama activity that Mr. Miller and this fourth grade class had, one becomes aware of structure, of steps, of stages of development in executing this technique. Mr. Miller knew how to build for a successful creative drama session. The steps he followed were these:

1. Select a good story for creative drama and then tell it.
2. With the class, break the plot down into sequences, or scenes, that can be played. Note these on the chalkboard.
3. From those noted on the board, choose a scene, or scenes, to be played.
4. Break the scene, or scenes, into further sequence.
5. Discuss the scene or scenes. Discuss setting, motivation, characterization, the times, physical makeup of the characters, etc. Help the children to develop mental images of the characters, what they did, how they did it, why they did it.
6. Choose the players. Let them go into conference and plan in more detail what they will do during the playing period.
7. Plan with the youngsters who remain. Let them know that the play will be re-cast and re-played, and that they might pretend a part in the next playing.
8. Instruct youngsters to watch the play for *five* things they like and *five* things that could be improved in the next playing.
9. With an agreed upon signal, start the play. Let it continue until finished.
10. Let players return to group, and all evaluate the play, using the criteria in #8.
11. Re-cast, instruct remaining students as in #8, and re-play the scene.
12. Evaluate. If time permits, re-cast and re-play.

STEP 1. Select a Good Story for Creative Drama and Then Tell It.

Mr. Miller made a wise choice when he told the old French tale, *Stone Soup*. That kind of story is best for creative drama activity. It contains high action, with few main characters, the plot structure is easy to follow, and it allows for ease of restructuring, episode by episode, or scene by scene.

Most folktales offer these built-in features. It is a wise leader who knows where to find these tales that can serve as a genesis for creative drama. A hunt through most folktale anthologies will reveal many stories that offer rich experiences with this technique. Specific sources to which one might turn for story selection would be, among others, the following:

BURGER, I. *Creative Play Acting.* Cranbury, N.J.: A. S. Barnes & Co., Inc., n.d.

FITZGERALD, BURDETTE. *Let's Act the Story.* Palo Alto: Fearon Publishers, Inc., 1957.

———. *World Tales for Creative Dramatics.* Englewood Cliffs, N. J.: Prentice-Hall, Inc., 1962.

LEASE and SIKS. *Creative Dramatics in Home, School and Community.* New
York: Harper & Brothers, 1952.
SIKS, GERALDINE BRAIN. *Children's Literature for Dramatization.* New York:
Harper & Row Publishers, 1964.
WARD, W. *Playmaking with Children.* New York: Appleton-Century-Crofts,
1957.
———. *Stories to Dramatize.* Children's Theatre Press, 1952.

The telling of the story needs to be done with skill, if not real
artistry. All of the techniques and powers of a good storyteller need to
be employed in telling the story in as effective a way as possible.

The story, and the way it is told, are the raw materials from which
the creative drama is built. The imagery, the characterizations, the motivations, etc. in the playing period start in the telling and the hearing of
the story. It needs to be told by a storyteller-teacher who knows the
techniques of storytelling and one who knows how to employ those
techniques in the telling of the story.

STEP 2. With the Class, Break the Plot Down into Sequences, or Scenes, That Can Be Played. Note These on the Chalkboard.

When the story has been told, and the possibility of creative drama
is evident, it is necessary to analyze the plot structure of the story to
find what part, or parts, will be played. It is best that this be a cooperative effort between the students and the teacher. Undoubtedly, it would
be easier if the teacher simply outlined the plot, but the educational
value in a practice of this kind is doubtful. Through proper questioning
and guidance, a satisfactory plot outline can be created through mutual
effort.

It is important that the students and the teacher consider this plot
outline in terms of episodes or scenes. Each episode or scene can be
played, and if they are all played from first to last, the entire tale is
retold in dramatic form. Children readily grasp the concept of scenes
or episodes. They see hundreds of stories told in this manner on television every year, and they find it not at all difficult to transfer what
they have experienced through television, in terms of method of communication, to a preparation for creative drama.

It is well to note this plot outline on the chalkboard so that the
children can see the progression of the plot line, episode by episode.
They may want to modify the outline once it has been completed. This
is fine. Let them do it.

STEP 3. From Those Noted on the Board, Choose a Scene, or Scenes, To Be Played.

When the plot outline has been completed, and all the scenes or
episodes, from first to last, have been noted on the chalkboard, it is then

time to choose what scene or scenes will be played. Time usually does not permit playing the entire story. Also, to plan and play an entire story would be a monumental undertaking, one that youngsters of elementary school age would find most difficult. It is best to limit the task for the youngsters.

The choice of the scene, or scenes, again should be a cooperative venture. The merits and the limitations of each scene should be discussed. Children very quickly know which scene or episode offers greatest possibilities for dramatization. It is likely that different scenes will be suggested by various class members. It is then a simple matter to vote by a show of hands to decide which scene they will do.

The teacher then erases the others from the board, leaving only the scene, or scenes, that will be played.

STEP 4. *Break the Scene, or the Scenes, into Further Sequence.*

Even though the children have outlined the plot structure of the story and have chosen the scene they will play, more analysis of the plot is needed before they can successfully launch into a creative drama experience. They need to find the sequence of events in the scene they have chosen. They need to know how the scene is constructed, what incidents go into the scene, what happened first, second, and so on.

Again, teacher guidance is an important variable. Mr. Miller's asking questions is a good example of a technique that usually elicits from children the sequential order of the scene to be played.

The teacher also should summarize the sequence of incidents in the scene, once they have been established. Some write it on the board, others prefer to do it orally. The method of summarizing usually depends upon the complexity of the scene sequence, or sequences. If it is complicated, it may be well to note the sequence on the board. If the sequence is not complicated, an oral summary is usually enough.

It is most important, however, that the youngsters have a clear idea of sequential order of the scene they will play. Without it, the play can flounder, or even fail.

STEP 5. *Discuss the Scene or Scenes. Discuss Setting, Motivation, Characterization, the Times, Physical Make-up of the Characters, Etc. Help the Children To Develop Mental Images of the Characters, What They Did, How They Did It, Why They Did It.*

The heart of any good experience in creative drama is the characterization that youngsters give to the people who, just a few moments ago, lived only in their imaginations as a storyteller told a tale. Now the children must transform these images into people who will be visible, and who will re-create a part of that story in the classroom. It is time to create characters, to understand them, to make them believable, to give flesh and blood to an abstraction.

Creative drama is not effective with sets, properties (a theatrical term meaning implements, tools, articles, etc. that are used in stage plays), costumes, make-up, sound effects, etc. These often detract from the effectiveness of the creative drama. It is easier to imagine these material details rather than try to use a "reasonable facsimile." A youngster can mentally create the costume of a soldier of the Napoleonic Wars more easily than he can put on a pseudo-soldier outfit and pretend it is not what it really is. Costumes and properties often cause giggles and extraneous disturbance because children tend to find themselves and each other very funny when they are "dressed up," and they *are* funny. It's best to leave the costumes to Hallowe'en where they belong. Children's imaginations are far better than any costume, property, or make-up that can be offered.

Children can create these characters, show how they look, interpret their behavior, etc. best by talking about them. With proper guidance, the teacher can elicit from the youngsters their own creation of the characters. The mind's eye can see so much more than can the natural eye if given the proper opportunities.

All children will not agree on the characterizations. Some may have an entirely different interpretation of the character, how he looks, and why he behaves as he does. This is well and good. (Interpretation of literature should never be a rigid exercise in conformity.) If there is disagreement, the several playings of the scene can offer just as many different concepts of a particular character. How much richer the youngsters' literary awareness will be because of this.

When questioning children about the characterization they are creating, it is often well to relate the action and motivations of the character to their own experiences. Mr. Miller asked the children if "any of them had ever tried to fool someone." A question of this type could open the gate to a discussion about personal relationships to the characters in the story. The resulting analysis of characterization is bound to have depth.

As part of their preparation for play, many effective leaders of creative drama ask pupils to use single words to describe the characters. A teacher might ask the children to use a color to describe the character. A happy character may best be described as yellow or green, an angry character as red, and so on. Or the teacher may ask for a one-word description of a personality. Words such as *tricky, gay, bold, mean, happy, evil, sly, ugly,* etc. will tumble forth. Each word adds dimension to the understanding of the character, and will aid the player when he helps to create the drama.

Likewise, it is well to describe the characters physically. Is the character tall, short, fat, thin? Is he dark or fair? How does he walk? Show us. How can we pretend to be this person? What hints can we offer the player?

The setting is an important part of the preparation for the creative drama. What does the setting look like? What are the times? Is it early morning, afternoon, evening? Is the temperature or any other weather manifestation an important part in the setting?

Prepare a playing area . . . perhaps only by pushing desks or tables to one side. Establish where the doors are, where the characters will enter and exit. Determine carefully in advance where the necessary pieces of furniture or equipment (imaginary, of course) will be placed so that the players will be in agreement as to where certain action will take place. All of the scenery, of course, like the costumes, etc., are imaginary. Establishing where these imaginary settings are is most important, however.

With this background of information well-established, the children and the teacher are ready to move to #6.

STEP 6. Choose the Players. Let Them Go into Conference and Plan in More Detail What They Will Do During the Playing Period.

Choosing players is usually a simple task, because the teacher makes the selections. This may seem, to some, to be an excessively teacher-directed practice. In terms of time-economy, however, it is a necessity. To go through the selection process by class nominating, voting, etc., would take a great deal of time that would have to be subtracted from the activity itself, and so it seems best that the teacher make the selection.

Furthermore, when the players are chosen by the teacher, their needs, abilities, etc., which are known to him, are put to good use. He knows that the excessively shy child should never be put into a leading role, that it is better to have him play a supporting role or even just to watch until his confidence is built up enough to let him try a major part. The aggressive child, or the child with an abundance of confidence and leadership qualities, may find a secondary role a very valuable experience. The teacher knows it is good to have this child learn to follow as well as lead.

Many times during the first playing, or particularly when children are becoming familiar with the technique of creative drama, the teacher will select children who he knows will have a successful experience with the technique because he wants to set an example for other children to follow. The basic tenets of group dynamics support the practice of teacher-selection of the players for a session with creative drama.

After the players are chosen, they should be permitted a planning session of their own. They should be allowed to go into conference among themselves, away from the larger group, to plan in greater detail exactly what they will do and how they will do it. This is preparatory for the playing itself. It is a brief orientation period for the players before they start the playing. Five minutes or so, is usually adequate time for this planning.

STEP 7.   *Plan with the Youngsters Who Remain. Let Them Know That the Play Will Be Re-cast and Re-played, and that They Might Pretend a Part in the Next Playing.*

It is important always to assure the youngsters who were not se-lected to play roles, and who had wished to do so, that they will per-haps have a turn next time. They very likely will watch the playing period with keener eyes if they know that the next playing may include them.

It is well, also, to prepare children for watching live dramatic activity. For the most part, youngsters have experienced only mass-produced, "canned" drama activity on television and in the movie houses. They often don't know how to respond to a live performance. Several pointers from the teacher concerning this is in order.

Some successful leaders of creative drama activity will ask young-sters to watch for a particular point in order to guide their attention. This is particularly valuable with very young children, but is not always necessary with older ones.

STEP 8.   *Instruct Youngsters to Watch the Play for Five Things They Like and Five Things that Could Be Improved in the Next Playing.*

In order to sharpen the children's attention toward the play, and to base the evaluation of the play on sound criticism, this step is most important. The directions are given to the waiting audience while the players are still planning.

It is most important to ask youngsters pointedly to watch for two reasons, one to find what is good, and one to look for flaws that can be criticized in a way that will improve the play. These directions help children learn that "to criticize" does not mean "to tear apart" a product or an idea. It helps them understand that, instead, when one evaluates, it is best to do it in a positive way . . . where one builds rather than destroys.

Asking children to watch for five items in both contexts gives them an opportunity to watch for specifics in the total scheme of the play. It prevents their making one or two large generalizations which lack the specifics that are needed in a good evaluation. To watch for five items in each context is not arbitrary. If the teacher requests four, or even three items in each context, the quality of evaluation should not be affected.

STEP 9. *With an Agreed Upon Signal, Start the Play. Let It Continue Until Finished.*

Once the directions to the audience have been given, it is time to ask the players to begin. Five minutes or so are usually taken up in giving directions to the audience. This should be ample time for the players to plan.

It is not unusual for the players to hesitate and then request a few more minutes to plan. The acceptance or rejection of this request is the prerogative of the teacher. Most often, however, pupils won't need extra time, and the players will take their positions, ready for the creative drama. The teacher signals the start (a nod of his head or a quietly given oral signal, etc.), and the playing time begins. The teacher, of course, joins the audience and enjoys the play.

Even if mistakes are made as the play progresses, the teacher should not interfere. The playing should continue until pupils consider it is finished. The mistakes, the problems that can develop in the playing, will be evaluated later, and should be handled by the peer group.

If, however, the status of a child is at stake because of an honest error or an unforeseen problem, the teacher must rescue the child from embarrassment. There are times when a child may block or freeze and is unable to continue the play. This places him in a very awkward position and he may become subject to ridicule by the other children. At such times, of course, the teacher must interrupt the play. A youngster's ego needs are far more important than the successful playing of a scene with creative drama. These instances, however, are very rare.

Should giggling and nonsense behavior occur among the players, the teacher would be wise not to step in and stop the play. Most often, this behavior is a manifestation of embarrassment, and the child will soon recover and continue. The pressures from his peer group, at any rate, will be much more effective than the pressure from the teacher.

More often than not, the playing period will proceed smoothly. Children enjoy dramatic activity of this kind and will work hard to have a successful experience with it.

When the action has been completed and the scenes have been played, the teacher can interrupt quietly and stop the play. He can simply stand and say quietly, "Thank you very much. It was very good." The players will know that the play has ended and will return to their chairs.

STEP 10.   Let Players Return to Group, and All Evaluate the Play,
          Using the Criteria in #8.

When the players have returned to their chairs, it is time to begin the evaluation of the drama. This most important step is a preparation for the second playing as well as an important activity that will increase the children's facility with evaluation and their sharpness for perception.

This evaluation should be teacher-led. The teacher should structure the discussion so that the points that the children liked about the play are discussed before the points that they think could be improved in the next playing are discussed.

The teacher's attitude toward the drama will often set the stage for the evaluation. Most successful leaders of creative drama will comment about the play before the evaluative discussion begins. It is good, of course, to make a positive statement about it. If the teacher shows his enjoyment for and appreciation of an activity of this nature, it has, for all intents and purposes, received "official sanction." A sincere and deserved compliment to the players is a very productive way to start the evaluative discussion.

The teacher's role in the evaluation of the creative drama is that of augmenting and clarifying, of keeping the evaluation to pertinent points and discouraging cruel or unfair criticism. Sometimes the teacher will ask a youngster to "show again" how he had created a certain piece of action, or he will point out a certain bit of action that created good imagery. When the evaluation has run its course (approximately ten to fifteen minutes), the teacher stops the discussion and moves to #11.

STEP. 11.   Re-cast, Instruct Remaining Students as in #8 and, Re-play
          the Scene.

When the evaluation is complete and the teacher and students are satisfied that they can do the scene again, but with new insight and greater facility, it is time to re-cast and re-play.

The teacher again chooses the cast. This cast is a new one with no members from the first group of players. They are instructed to go to one side and plan their drama as did the first group. They are told that if they wish to change the imaginary scenery, they may do so by explaining it before they start.

The teacher, as in #7 and #8, directs the remaining youngsters as to how they are to watch the play. He again asks that they watch for five things they like about the play, and five things they would change to make the play a better one.

When the class has received its instructions and the players have planned, the drama is begun. It should be allowed to play until it is finished, after which the players return to their seats.

STEP 12.   Evaluate. If Time Permits, Re-cast and Re-play.

When the play has been completed, and the players have rejoined the class, it is again time to evaluate. The same procedure that was used in #10 should be used again.

The teacher can expect, and will usually find, that the second playing is a great improvement over the first, and that the second evaluation shows must more insight than did the first evaluation. Real depth analysis will often occur in the second evaluation session.

If time permits, re-cast, re-play, and evaluate. More than three playings in one day, however, is too many. Children tire of the activity, and its value decreases sharply.

POINTS FOR DISCUSSION AND THINGS TO DO

1. Choose from among the many folktales, three, in addition to those listed in the textbook, that are good for creative drama. Prepare them for telling and for a session with creative drama.
2. With your class, structure a folktale into scenes that will be good for dramatization. Discuss which scene, or scenes, would be best for playing. Using the twelve steps described in this chapter, have a creative drama experience with your class.
3. Why is creative drama not Theatre for Children?
4. What is the difference between creative drama and dramatic play? Role playing? Socio-drama?
5. Why is it good not to provide costumes, make-up, properties, etc. to children engaged in a creative drama?
6. What part does storytelling play in the making of a creative drama?
7. What classroom variables are needed before creative drama can be successful? Why are these variables important? How can teachers provide these variables?
8. Prepare a bibliography of good tales that can result in creative drama.

chapter 9

educational implications for creative drama

While creative drama is admittedly a delightful and fun-filled activity, can we as teachers possibly justify it as a regular part of our school program? Can we who have the grave responsibility of helping children learn the many skills, controls, and academic requirements that are a regular, (and many times legal) part of our school duties, provide time for such an activity? Without question, the answer is yes. The opportunities for learning as a result of interacting with creative drama technique are varied and impressive. The teacher who employs creative drama should know some of the more obvious implications for learning that creative drama can foster. The following discussion reveals some of the most evident educational advantages contained in this technique.

1. *Literary Analysis.* Certainly, one of the most apparent values of creative drama is the opportunity it affords children to analyze children's literature in depth, and at their own level. The preparation for and the execution and the evaluation of the creative drama experience *is* literary analysis.

It is unfortunately true that elementary school children oftentimes do not have experiences that will allow them to analyze their literature except when they write "book reports." While teachers often encourage the reading of trade books and provide many of these books for children to read, little chance is given to youngsters to analyze and discuss in real depth the plot structure, the characterization, the motivations, and the literary techniques employed by the writers of children's books. Huck and Kuhn, in their fine book, *Children's Literature in the Elementary School,* summarize this situation by stating: "The majority of elementary schools in the United States have no planned literature program; usually

Aperture Limited of California, Inc., Stockton, California   John Adams Elementary School Stockton, California

The skills of literary analysis are important in planning for creative drama. These skills are often transferred to the child's reading habits.

literature is subsumed under the 'reading' or 'English' programs."[1] Literary education in the elementary school is the poorer because of this lack.

The techniques employed with creative drama present one way to fill this gap. Children become acutely aware of literary analysis and interpretation when they prepare, execute, and evaluate a creative drama experience. They need this awareness if the creative drama is to be a success. They should know plot structure; they should understand the sequence of events; and they should understand the characters, motivations, the setting, etc. before they can dramatize. They will offer interpretations, and they will relate the experiences in the story and in the subsequent dramatization to their own life experiences, thus bringing additional dimensions to the story through analysis.

---

[1]Charlotte S. Huck and Doris Young Kuhn, *Children's Literature in the Elementary School*, 2d ed. (New York: Holt, Rinehart & Winston, Inc., 1968), p. 649.

Literary analysis, an area too long neglected in the elementary school, is emphasized in the experience with creative drama. Its educational value, from that one aspect, makes creative drama an important technique to be employed in the language arts curriculum.

2. *The Listening Skills.* Helping children learn to listen is an educational objective that most teachers value. It seems that children, living in a world of noise as they do, have learned to protect themselves from that noise by simply "tuning it out." One result, of course, is that in this "tuning out process," children frequently have not learned "when to tune in." Many youngsters have not learned to distinguish that which should be heard from that which is not important. The learning process depends greatly upon children's ability to listen. When they don't know how to listen, difficulties are bound to result.

The problem of developing listening skills in children has demanded scholarly research which has resulted in a wealth of written materials concerning the problem. This research has indicated time and time again, that in order to develop the skills of listening, children need to be structured as to what they will be listening for, and how to listen. In short, they must be given directions so that they will know not only that they must listen, but also why it is important that they do so.

Creative drama provides such an opportunity. Children eagerly listen to a good storyteller. When they know that creative drama may result from the telling, and they realize their responsibility in building for the play, their listening has been structured, and they know the reasons for their listening.

They know that their responsibility includes re-creating the story in sequential order and breaking the scene they have chosen into further sequence; that it includes listening to their peers and to the teacher while the characterization, motivation, and scene design are being discussed so that they can agree, or disagree with the comments, particularly if they are to play a role. They know that the teacher will ask them to watch (and listen) for the ten points of criticism that will come in the evaluation of the play.

All stages of development and evaluation of a creative drama activity demand the use of good listening skills. Learning theory has told us that children will learn best when they can see the immediate use for what they are to learn. Creative drama provides an opportunity for children to put what they've heard to that immediate use.

The listening skills, which so often are poorly developed, can be enhanced and even learned when children experience creative drama activity. Without good listening skills, the activity cannot be successful.

3. *Oral Language.* The development of oral language is a major goal of the elementary school curriculum. As educators, we know that

the reading and the writing vocabulary are, to a large extent, dependent upon the speaking vocabulary. Children cannot read and write if they do not have a speaking (and listening) vocabulary. It is, therefore, important that children be given many opportunities to use oral language in order to develop that very necessary vocabulary.

Creative drama is not a passive activity. It demands action, and it demands oral language . . . and lots of it. Children must use a great deal of oral language in preparing, executing, and evaluating a creative drama session. They use oral language in several ways.

One way children use spoken words, phrases, and sentences in an experience of this kind is in isolating structure, noting sequence, and finding exactly "what is" in the re-creation of the story. Language is used also in a creative, descriptive sense. Words are needed to describe scenery, to tell about emotions, to paint symbolic pictures. Oral language is used in a dramatic context, too, where words and their delivery are most important in the execution of the drama. Oral language in this context must be distinct and easy to understand. This is obvious to children who participate in creative drama.

The oral skills of discussion, planning, and evaluation are given opportunities to develop when creative drama is at work. Oral language is the heart of this technique.

As an experience that will develop and foster oral language, the technique of creative drama has few equals. The growth of effective oral language is very noticeable, and often spectacular, when children are given the rich experiences inherent in creative drama.

4. *Creative Thinking.* If oral language is the heart of this technique, then creative thinking is its blood. The entire process operates under the imaginative, creative powers of its participants.

The act of imagining, of pretending, is basic to a successful session with creative drama. Youngsters are given a stimulus: The Story. From that point on, the creative process operates.

How do the characters look? How do they behave? How can we describe them? Each of these questions requires a creative response. How does the scenery look? Where is the table? How large is the room? These questions demand creation also.

Children do not use costumes, properties, scenery, etc. in creative drama. All of these variables in the drama must be created in the imaginations of the players and of those who watch. Characterizations, costumes, and scenery that are created for one playing can change and be quite different in the next playing. It's easy. All it takes is a shift of the imagination.

Creative thinking implies divergent thinking. There are many ways to see a character and his motivation in creative drama. Is Cinderella blonde? To some, she may be a brunette. Who is correct? Obviously, either is correct. Divergency and creativity are inseparable. In a creative experience such as one with this technique, creativity and divergency are fostered and encouraged.

The development of the creative potential that is in all people is becoming a major issue with curriculum workers. They know the value of working toward this goal. The technique of creative drama offers one very fine way of developing this precious human resource.

5. *Planning: From Abstract to Concrete.* It is difficult for children to take an abstract idea and develop that idea, step by step, into a concrete reality. The planning, and the successful execution of those plans toward the desired result, demands a high level of thinking and acting. The education of children must provide opportunities for children to learn the values and skills of planning that will develop an abstract idea into a reality. Knowing how to plan and how to execute those plans is an important part of childhood education.

The planning periods in a creative drama activity offer youngsters a primary, firsthand experience with taking an abstract idea, and through planning, arriving at a final, concrete product. The steps in creating a drama require real planning. The final result, the drama itself, does not come about through accident. It comes about through careful planning, execution of those plans, and evaluation.

Each stage, beyond the actual telling of the story, requires children's planning. The structuring of the story into scenes, the choosing of the scene to play, the breaking of the selected scene into further segments, the discussion of the characters, motivations, scenery, etc., and the final small group planning, as well as the directions for watching and the ultimate playing and evaluating of the play, all help children understand the value of structuring and planning.

The teacher, the leader of the creative drama activity, would be wise to help children know that the play will stand or fall on the merits of the plans. If, at some time, the play should not go well, or if the children's evaluation of the play should miss the issue of planning, the teacher would be wise to point out that perhaps the plans were at fault. He can help his pupils know that the planning session is the foundation of creative drama. If the foundation is weak, the structure built from it will often topple and fall.

Children can learn quickly the techniques of planning for a creative drama. They know the stages and move from one to another with amazing ease and skill. When this happens, children have learned a very valuable process. The teacher can then help them transfer this skill into other areas.

Helping children learn to plan, to take an idea and develop it, step by step, into a reality is an important part of the teaching-learning act.

Creative drama done with skill and care, can help children learn this valuable process.

6. *The Skills of Effective Evaluation.* The skills of effective evaluation are important skills to learn. Unfortunately, children many times think that evaluation or criticism means that one finds "what is wrong" or "the bad things" about a product or effort. Criticism then becomes a negative, destructive activity with the questionable values of tearing down and destroying as its only assets. Instead, criticism and evaluation, if they are to be valuable, should imply constructive activity . . . activity that will strengthen and improve a product or an idea. Effective evaluation needs to be positive, not negative, if the evaluation is to do anything but destroy. It is important to help children know that criticism is a positive activity, that it is a valuable step in developing an idea, and that it represents a high level of productive thinking.

Evaluation (and, therefore, the development of the skills of evaluation) is an important part of building for creative drama. Children are expected to evaluate the drama and are specifically asked to do so. The directions for evaluation, however, are designed so that positive criticism will result, criticism that is geared to improve the product, not to destroy it. Step 8, as outlined in Chapter 8 of this book, is concerned with the children's watching the play for five things they like and five things that can be improved in the next playing. These directions clearly imply positive, constructive criticism.

With teacher assistance and guidance, the evaluation session of the creative drama experience can be a very valuable learning situation. It can be a time when pupils learn that effective evalution is a positive activity; a time for them to learn how to criticize from a positive viewpoint so that the product or idea being criticized is, in fact, made stronger as a result of the criticisms.

Implications for Education

It should be evident, from the six points discussed above, that creative drama does have significant implications for education. It should also be evident that this technique, as a regular part of the elementary school curriculum, can be justified. Creative drama offers opportunities for certain kinds of learning, opportunities that are difficult to equal with other techniques. As a way of helping children learn, creative drama does have an important part in the ongoing classroom program.

The six points of educational value inherent in creative drama as offered in this chapter should in no way imply that they are the only points of educational value inherent in this technique. The opposite is quite true. Creative drama offers a wide spectrum of educational opportunities to the creative teacher who will seek them.

The application of creative drama to the area of social studies, for instance, offers an entirely new dimension to the technique. To play scenes depicting life on a wagon train moving west, family life in another culture, Pilgrim life in New England, the job of the postman, the fireman, etc. will bring additional insight and adventure into the social studies program. The same is true of science, music, and other areas of the curriculum. The same basic technique of creative drama is used, but the stimulus (the story) changes to a more academic concept.

Pretending at play is a natural part of childhood. To structure that play and convert it into a learning experience is a valid educational practice.

Points for Discussion and Things To Do

1. Review the educational implications outlined in this chapter. Which seems most valuable? Why? Discuss this with other students and defend your point of view.
2. What other educational implications that were not included in this chapter does this technique have? List them. Compare them with your classmates' lists.
3. Will all children's literature lend itself to creative drama? Why? or Why not?
4. Despite the fact that creative drama does not attempt to be a technique that fosters psychological or sociological learning, are there implications for this kind of learning in creative drama? How?
5. Discuss this technique with a successful classroom teacher. What educational implications does he see in this technique?
6. Creative drama is a "fun" activity. Does the "fun" aspect detract from its educational value? Why? or Why not?
7. How can creative drama be justified in a lesson plan? Prepare a lesson plan and justify its value.
8. Find an incident in a social studies textbook, or an adventure in a trade book, that deals with social studies concepts. Prepare it for creative drama. Tell the story and have a creative drama session. Tell why learning has been enhanced because of the experience.
9. Find an incident in the life of a famous scientist, musician, artist, historical figure, or contemporary personage that will make a good creative drama. Use a well-written biography for your source. Prepare it for creative drama. What new insights will children gain as a result of this experience?

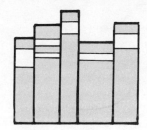

selected
references

ARBUTHNOT, MAY HILL. *Children and Books.* 3d ed. Chicago: Scott, Foresman & Company, 1964.

BAMMAN, HENRY A. et al. *Oral Interpretation of Children's Literature.* Dubuque, Iowa: Wm. C. Brown Company Publishers, 1964.

CARLSON, BERNICE W. *Act it Out.* New York: Abingdon Press, 1965.

FITZGERALD, BURDETTE S. *Let's Act the Story.* Palo Alto: The Fearon Publishers, Inc., 1957.

CROSSCUT, RICHARD. *Children and Dramatics.* New York: Charles Scribner's Sons, 1966.

HUCK CHARLOTTE S., and KUHN, DORIS YOUNG. *Children's Literature in the Elementary School.* New York: Holt, Rinehart & Winston, Inc., 1968.

LEASE, RUTH, and SIKS, GERALDINE B. *Creative Dramatics in Home, School, and Community.* New York: Harper, 1952.

SIKS, GERALDINE B. *Creative Drama, An Art for Children.* New York: Harper, 1958.

———, ed. *Children's Literature for Dramatization: An Anthology.* New York: Harper & Row, Publishers, 1964.

MENAGH, H. BERESFORD. *Creative Dramatics in Guiding Children's Language Learning.* Edited by Pose Lamb. Dubuque, Iowa: Wm. C. Brown Company Publishers, 1967.

WALKER, PAMELA PRINCE. *Seven Steps to Creative Children's Dramatics.* New York: Hill & Wang, Inc., 1957.

WAY, BRIAN. *Development through Drama.* London: Longmans, Green and Co., Ltd. 1967.

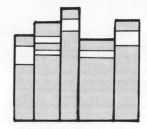

index

Date Due